THE BASIC BOOK OF SEA KAYAKING

"Almost anyone can get into a kayak and paddle happily toward the horizon. If you want to make a habit of coming back in one piece, take a cruise through *The Basic Book of Sea Kayaking*. Whether it's getting out on the water or getting back to the beach, Derek can point you in the right direction."

—*Sea Kayaker* magazine

"Anyone who has cast a wistful eye toward a sea kayak will through this book find a way into a kayak and onto the sea. Well done!"

—*Canoe & Kayak* magazine

A FALCON GUIDE®

HOW TO PADDLE SERIES

THE BASIC BOOK OF
Sea Kayaking
SECOND EDITION

DEREK C. HUTCHINSON

FALCONGUIDES®

GUILFORD, CONNECTICUT
HELENA, MONTANA

AN IMPRINT OF THE GLOBE PEQUOT PRESS

A **FALCON** GUIDE ®

Falcon and FalconGuides are registered trademarks of Morris Book Publishing, LLC.

Interior photos: Photo on page vi by Robert Shertz, courtesy of Derek Hutchinson. Photo on page x © photos.com. All other photos courtesy of Derek Hutchinson.

Illustrations: All illustrations by Derek Hutchinson. Illustrations on pages 41, 42, 43, 44, 45, 46, 49, 50, 51, 52, 53, 54, 55, 56, 57, 58, 60, 61, 62, 63, and 64 by Derek Hutchinson and reprinted from *The Complete Book of Sea Kayaking* with permission from A&C Black (publishers) Limited, London, England.

Spot photography throughout by Derek Hutchinson

Text design by Nancy Freeborn

Library of Congress Cataloging-in-Publication Data is available.

ISBN: 978-0-7627-4283-7

Manufactured in China
Second Edition/First Printing

To Paul and Bethan,
who have both felt the magic of the paddle.

The author steadies Jane Mrowka as she demonstrates one of the basic confidence exercises.

Contents

Preface

Very little has changed in sea kayaking since I launched the first edition of this little book upon the unsuspecting public. A few items, however, needed mentioning to bring the book up to date.

I have added information on the wing paddle, polycarbonate kayaks, and inflatable kayaks. I've shared with the reader what I consider the ultimate in kayaking footwear. Most important of all, I have dealt with a certain type of craft that has appeared in recent years under the misleading heading of recreational boat, also known as near shore boat, or NSB, along with some timely warnings to those attracted to this kind of boat.

Sea kayaking is a social sport and the best way possible to experience the natural beauty of the coastline.

Introduction

So you have decided to try the sport of sea kayaking. Well, let me say that you've made a good choice. In the years to come, you will delight in the freedom that the solo sea kayak gives you. No other craft in the world will offer you a greater intimacy with the water. I remember as if it were yesterday how I felt when I sat in a solo kayak for the very first time. I had been in a rowing boat many times, so I felt at home on the water. The kayak, however, had quite a different feel. I didn't feel safe at all. The first time I sat in it, I felt wobbly. Even the slightest shift of weight made me feel as if I were going to capsize. I knew I was never going to be any good at this. How could anyone in their right mind go out to sea in anything as unstable as this? It took about ten minutes of paddling around in circles, under the watchful eye of a qualified coach, for me to gradually relax my white-knuckle death-grip on the paddle and my nervous system. I suddenly realized that I could do two things at once. I discovered the joy of being able to paddle *and look around* at the same time. I also discovered that death did not immediately follow after the first capsize. Mind you, I didn't like the cold water, but this problem was soon solved when I was introduced to one of the early wet suits.

As yet you probably do not have a kayak of your own, but let us look into the future and anticipate some of the things you might like to do. Will you, for instance, paddle up quiet estuaries on day trips and study the wildlife with your camera? Perhaps you are conscious of your body's needs and are the type who likes to paddle fast and get a good workout. Of course, for the competitive and the superathletic, racing may be the answer. At some time most paddlers like to fill their boats with camping gear and take off to wild and wondrous places. You will be delighted to know that any or all of these options are open to you. The choice is yours.

The origins of kayaking on the sea go back thousands of years, but you will be glad to know that little has really changed. Boats may now be made of modern materials, and the rest of your equipment may be high-tech—and, of course, unlike the Inuit, you'll be able to swim and you'll wear a life jacket. But apart from that, the sea is still the sea and the wind is still the enemy. These age-old elements will always be with us. Because of this, I will try in this book to deal with some general elements of basic seamanship as well as the basic strokes and deepwater rescue techniques.

As the author of a beginner's how-to-do-it book, I possess impeccable credentials. I have paddled with the wrong people, in the wrong boat, in the wrong weather, in the wrong place and at the wrong time, and with the wrong equipment. I have probably made every mistake there is to make. Yes, I know what you are going to say, but on December 4, 1966, I nearly drowned and was resuscitated. Does that now qualify me?

I have now passed through this vale of tears. I have done all the research, and although I still make errors from time to time, they are now less frequent and less life-threatening.

During the course of this book, I shall be both giving instructions and making recommendations regarding strokes, rescues, equipment, and perhaps certain courses of action. To save you the agony of reinventing the broken wheel, and giving you the dilemma of scores of difficult options, I shall merely tell you of *my* preference and what *I* would do in certain circumstances. With experience, however, you will discover—to your delight or frustration—that no matter what aspect you choose in sea kayaking, you will usually be faced with a number of safe and workable options.

As your circle of sea kayaking friends widens, you may find that some of them have "gone native" and favor the narrow Greenland-style kayaks made from wood and canvas. They may even prefer to use the narrow paddles modeled on those from the same area. Well, most experienced paddlers have at one time or another experimented in this way, and this choice will eventually be open to you. At beginner level, however, my advice is to learn the basic paddling techniques with equipment of modern design, using modern techniques, and save choices like this until farther down the road of experience. Be patient and you will be surprised how quickly the time will arrive when you will be making your own judgments—and, naturally, your own mistakes. Until that happy time, let me advise you and try to keep you dry.

CHAPTER ONE

Basic Equipment: What Do I Need?

KAYAK CONSTRUCTION

Let us presume that you now want to go ahead with the idea of kayaking on the sea or open water and you wish to purchase a suitable craft. Before you face the minefield of the retail store, let me give you some information that will help you.

Fiberglass Kayaks

The most popular method of construction is GRP (Glassfiber Reinforced Plastic). This is usually shortened to *fiberglass*. The word *composite* is also becoming more popular, because it covers a wider range of materials.

A fiberglass kayak is made from two molds: one for the hull and one for the deck. These molds are covered first with wax and then with a release agent. A colored resin gel coat is sprayed onto the inside of the mold. It is this gel coat that gives the kayak its smooth, high-gloss surface finish. Once this gel coat has started to "cure" (harden), sheets of fiberglass are laid into the mold and impregnated with polyester resin. Most manufacturers have their own favorite layup of unwoven glass matted together with the coarser lay up of woven-roving. If this process, known as laying up, is carefully and professionally done, there should be no air bubbles in the finished product. Boats that are laid up by hand tend to soak up slightly more resin. This gives them a little added weight, but this thicker gel, added to the lower part of the hull, helps to protect the hull from damage when boats are dragged over rocks or rough surfaces.

The other method of laying up the fiberglass is known as vacuum-bagging. The mold is prepared in the manner previously described. It is then covered by a large, transparent plastic sheet. This is done immediately after the resin has been pumped in and is still in liquid form. A seal is made around the edge of the mold, and the air is then sucked out by vacuum pipes. Working by hand from the outside, through the heavy-duty plastic sheet, it is possible to spread the resin evenly throughout the mold.

Vacuum-bagged kayaks finish up lighter than those laid up by hand. Although the insides are smoother, they tend to be more flexible and so need to be reinforced in certain areas.

Once the layup has been allowed to "cure" or set in the molds, the two halves are joined together with an internal seam consisting of a strip of resin-soaked glass or glass tape. Sometimes an external seam is formed by a gunwale strip for added strength. Some manufacturers favor joining their boats with a plastic extrusion. As well as joining the hull and deck together, the extrusion incorporates a hollow channel to take the rudder cables.

The cockpit coaming and seat unit are laid up as a separate unit and are fixed in place with resin putty.

The joy of a fiberglass kayak is that after purchase, it can be customized by the addition of extra bulkheads and hatches, recessed deck fittings, anchor points for tow and deck lines, knee tubes and compass wells, and other bits and pieces that make the nonkayaking months a time of innovation and experiment.

Kevlar Kayaks

Kevlar is an exceptionally strong and lightweight material used in the manufacture of bulletproof vests and shields. Kayaks that have Kevlar as their reinforcing cloth finish up lighter than those made of fiberglass. Because the lamination is thin, Kevlar boats tend to flex and may need stiffening supports. Kevlar boats are more difficult to repair if they get damaged, and they tend to be used mainly for racing craft where acceleration is important.

Polyethylene Kayaks

You will discover that plastic kayaks are cheaper to buy and are not as easily damaged as those made of fiberglass. The polyethylene used in the molding of plastic boats is either cross-linked or linear.

Cross-linked boats have a better resistance to impact, but because of their increased flexibility, they need supporting. They cannot be repaired by welding.

Linear polyethylene gives a stiffer construction and has a better resistance to abrasion. These boats can be repaired by welding during the early years of their life.

Although plastic kayaks have been a boon to outfitters and to those who rent boats, they are not indestructible. They can lose their shape in hot weather, and storing or carrying them without proper support can cause irreparable damage. Beware of the bulkheads in plastic kayaks that are fixed in place with any kind of adhesive. Glue does not take to polyethylene, and the integrity of a bulkhead secured in this way can be measured in months. Polyethylene kayaks also tend to be much heavier than composite kayaks, and their hulls do not glide over the surface of the water as easily as those of boats made of fiberglass.

Polycarbonate Kayaks

Polycarbonate, used in the manufacture of industrial protective goggles, is one of the newer materials in kayak construction yet not the most widespread. It has a more highly polished finish than polyethylene and from a distance cannot be distinguished from one of its shiny composite cousins. Although polycarbonate retains its rigidity and is more abrasion resistant than polyethylene, its resistance to crushing is not as high as that of polyethylene. Furthermore, polycarbonate is still more expensive than polyethylene. Some repairs to polycarbonate can be made using resin and fiberglass, but the material has not been around long enough for us to judge its long-term properties.

Folding Kayaks

If you intend to do a lot of traveling to places where your baggage space is restricted or expensive, then a folding kayak will solve your problem. Boats-in-a-bag are also handy if your storage space is limited—say, in a small apartment. If you enjoy cycling, you could even tow your bagged kayak on a trailer behind you. The downside is that folding boats are very expensive, they need maintenance, and, naturally, they take time to assemble.

Frames can be made of aluminum tubing or wood, held in place by frames of heavy-duty polyethylene or marine-grade plywood. Once assembled, the frame is covered by a skin of heavy-weight rubberized fabric. The strongest of these materials is known as Hyperlon.

Inflatable Kayaks

There was a time when seasoned paddlers did not take inflatable kayaks seriously, but in recent years, designs have become more sophisticated both in appearance and performance.

Like the folding kayak, the inflatable kayak can be stored at home, carried in the trunk of your car, or stored as luggage on an airplane. The best of these kayaks have a number of compartments that inflate separately. This means that all your eggs (air!) are not in one basket. The separate compartments also give the inflated skin the overall rigidity necessary for the boat to track (hold course) well and be paddled comfortably.

The outer skin is usually made of a durable rubber laminated onto a woven fabric. These outer skins can take a surprising amount of punishment, but it is always prudent to carry a repair kit, one that will repair the valves as well as the outer skin.

One of the best of this new generation of inflatable boats even has an extruded plastic cockpit coaming joined to the main hull that gives the sitting area a watertight seal when used with a standard-size spray skirt.

Because these kayaks are filled with air, they do not need hatches, bulkheads, or any kind of floatation. One particularly well designed model I have seen has canvas-covered front and rear decks around which are carefully placed grab lines. This boat is also fitted with loading hatches to help you access the extremities of the hull when packing gear.

The overall performance and speed of inflatables fall short of their hard-shell cousins. In mixed groups, therefore, inflatables may have difficulty keeping up. Depending on the amount of freeboard of your craft (the distance between the waterline and the deck), you may also have trouble controlling the boat in high winds. This problem can be eased somewhat by carrying heavy gear as ballast.

Wooden Kayaks

For the beginner, building your own wooden boat is often a good way to get started. There are kits on the market where all the difficult cutting operations have already been done for you. Personally, I love wooden boats, but the trouble is, I never feel I can run up onto rocks without a tear coming into my eye. If you do put a hole in your boat, you will find that repairs are difficult, time-consuming, and rarely invisible.

To get the best out of your wooden kayak, it should be dried out thoroughly after use, stored in a dry place, and maintained by rubbing down and varnishing at least once every two years. The frequency of varnishing will, of course, depend on the amount of use your boat gets.

Recreational Boats, or Near Shore Boats (NSBs)

The short, stubby recreational or near shore boat, with its huge, wide cockpit, is not a kayak in the true sense of the word. Most of these boats have flat bottoms, making them very stable on calm water. In windy weather, however, their high freeboard makes them difficult to control or keep on a straight course, and their lack of hull speed makes for slow headway against even a moderate current or tidal stream. Some recreational boats have no footrests, which can make forward paddling extremely tiring.

Ironically, it is the very stability of these craft that makes them so potentially dangerous. Many recreational boat owners think that the large cockpit has been designed to accommodate not only the paddler but a small child, a dog, a picnic box, a carton of drink containers, and the fishing tackle. This attitude is the kiss of death! The recreational boat's stability even encourages people to change places or kneel up in the cockpit to lean over and retrieve items that are out of reach. Any of the above activities increase the risk of a sudden capsize.

Because of their design, recreational boats are very limited in the type of journeys they can undertake. To keep the price low, manufacturers do not usually fit these craft with the safety features we have come to expect, such as spray skirts, watertight compartments or other types of buoyancy, grab-lines, or bow and stern toggles. The buoyancy/flotation supplied inside recreational boats is usually minimal. Some are fitted with a hatch and bulkhead in the rear section of the boat, but this is hardly a safety feature, as these boats are still prone to swamping and tend to float in the stern-in-the-air position.

Safety and Rescue in Recreational Boats

Caution: The "T" Rescue described in this book is only recommended for sea kayaks having watertight compartments at the front and rear, or adequate buoyancy of some other kind. I do not know of any assisted rescue that has a good chance of success with an upturned recreational boat in choppy, open water. The short length of these boats makes it difficult for a large cockpit to be lifted clear of the water during the first stage of the emptying procedure.

Recreational boats should *only* be used on enclosed water and within swimming distance of the shore. Wear an approved life vest (do *not* use it as a seat cushion) and dress in suitable immersion clothing at all times.

In the event of a capsize, *do not attempt to turn your boat upright again.* If you do, the boat may well swamp and sink. Take hold of the front toggle—if the boat has one—and tow the boat to shore, keeping it all the while in the inverted position. An upside-down hull will have enough air trapped inside it to keep you afloat during your swim. If you hold your paddle in the same hand as the toggle, you will have a free hand to help you with your swimming.

Never leave the boat to swim to shore. Stay with the upturned boat. You will have more chance of being seen and rescued.

Waving your paddle slowly to and fro in the air is an international distress signal. This is when you'll wish you'd painted your blades one of those eye-catching day-glow colors. If you anticipate a long stay in the water, tie yourself to the boat with a quick-release knot. If the boat does happen to sink, you must be able to free yourself quickly so you don't go down with it. On the other hand, if you become unconscious, you don't want to lose contact with it.

Flotation

Kayaks that for one reason or another fill with water either sink or become hopelessly unstable. This, of course, is dangerous. Back in 1974 I tried fitting bulkheads and thus created watertight compartments inside my Baidarka. The idea worked, and now most sea kayaks are manufactured with watertight bulkheads and hatches already fixed in place.

If your kayak does not have bulkheads, you will have to fill every available space with large, specially shaped buoyancy bags. These are placed well inside the boat, one in front of the footrest and the other behind the cockpit. They are then inflated in place by means of long tubes. Before pushing your bags into place, make sure that there are no jagged projections inside the hull of the boat or the bags will burst.

CHOOSING A KAYAK

There's no such thing as the perfect sea kayak, so you can stop looking now. As a designer, I have always been faced with a number of complex and frustrating problems. The kayak must be light enough for the frailest of paddlers to lift up onto the top of a vehicle, yet strong enough to withstand the batterings of rough usage. A kayak must run straight at all times—even in the most trying of conditions—yet turn easily when the need arises. It must be stable enough to give the timid confidence but versatile enough to allow bracing strokes to be performed easily. The hull must have enough space to accommodate a mountain of equipment, but the amount of *freeboard* (the area between the waterline and the gunwale line) must be kept to a minimum. High seats give extra speed but less stability. Low seats give stability but can also provide the paddler with wet elbows and skinned knuckles.

The worst piece of advice you'll get is to choose a boat that is comfortable for you. If you do that as a novice, you will naturally choose a kayak that feels immediately stable. This will be your first big mistake, because after a few hours of paddling, you will get used to the boat and suddenly it will be like paddling a barge. I would compare it to riding a bicycle fitted with training wheels. What you need is lots of "dry" runs in as many different models as you can manage.

Rent boats, and try out those belonging to your friends. Find out who is selling a kayak, not so you can buy theirs but to learn why they are selling it and which new model they are now going to buy and why!

If you want to check out the stability of a kayak, first adjust the footrests so that your legs are slightly bent. Sit in the boat and position yourself next to a dock. If no dock is available, use the kayak of a friend who is also on the water. What you are looking for is something solid to lean upon. Support the nearest hand lightly on the dock and lean slowly over. The knee on the high side should be bent upward and hooked underneath the cockpit coaming. The leg nearest the dock should be straight and pushing down on the footrest. As you start to lean, you should feel some resistance. This is what is known as *primary stability*, and it is what gives you that comfortable, secure feeling when you're paddling normally on flat water. Now lift your support hand a fraction of an inch above the dock and keep on leaning. You should be able to take the gunwale well over and into the water and still not have to support yourself. This is know as *secondary stability.* Suddenly, there will come a point when the boat will go over and there is nothing you can do with your body to prevent it. This is the *moment of capsize.*

As a little exercise, try wobbling the boat from side to side, to the limit of its secondary stability, using only your hips. Keep your hand poised above the dock, just in case. Keep on doing this for a few minutes. Through repetition the kayak's stability will be registered on your nervous system and the balance mechanism in your brain. Very soon your balance will be instinctive.

Remember that your skill level will start and improve the moment you sit in the boat. Don't think that width brings stability. A hull with a round cross section that is 25 inches wide will throw you upside down in seconds. On the other hand, a kayak that has good primary and secondary stability and is 22 inches wide will give you comfort and confidence even in rough seas.

All kayaks are *stable* when they are loaded. The most popular kayaks tend to be 20 to 24 inches wide and 15 to 18 feet long. Boats with a lot of *rocker* are easier to turn than straight-keeled boats. Straight-keeled kayaks have good directional stability.

What to Look For

To familiarize yourself with the general layout of a sea kayak, take time to look at the illustration (fig. 1-1) on page 9.

1. **Toggles.** Look at the end toggles; these should be at the extremities of the kayak. Toggles are not just for carrying. If you ever need to be towed, this will be where the tow line will be fastened, so the loops must be strong. After a capsize you will need to hold onto the toggle and tow your boat ashore. If you

capsize in surf or broken water, the kayak must be *able to rotate* while you still retain hold of the toggle. Look especially at the rear toggle. If the kayak is fitted with a rudder, would you be able to hang on to the kayak without being injured as the boat rotates?

2. **Deck lines.** Deck lines should be taut but allow you to get your fingers underneath. The fittings that secure the deck lines should be recessed. Fittings that are not recessed but stand higher than deck level can shred knuckles and spray skirts during capsize recovery drills.

3. **The foredeck.** Steeply pitched foredecks do not hold charts well, and it's often difficult to position a compass flat in the center of the deck. Certain paddle strokes are influenced if the deck is too high.

4. **Hatches.** Hatches should be watertight. Round and oval ones are very good, but I'm afraid you take your chances with hatches of any other shape. Beware of those hatches that have lids over neoprene seals. People tend to remove the rubber seals during storage and then forget to replace them before going onto the water. Check inside the hatch rim to see that the rim has been fitted properly and that the finish is smooth. You should not be able to feel any ragged strands of glass. Be careful when you do this.

5. **Seats.** The seat pan should cradle your behind without cutting off the blood supply to your legs. Your thighs should be comfortable and not nipped too tight. When you are sitting on the seat, your knees should be able to fit under the cockpit coaming or under custom-made thigh braces.

   When it comes to seat backs, *backstraps* are flexible, comfortable, and adjustable. In contrast, rigid *backrests* held in place by small pieces of cord and elastic tend to have a mind of their own and always seem to dislodge at the worst possible time. Also, high rigid backrests can prevent you from doing a number of Eskimo Rolls.

6. **Cockpit coaming.** Check to see if the edge has been sanded smooth. The edges of thin sharp cockpit coamings can damage spray skirts. A thick edge gives a better seal than a thin one.

7. **Bulkheads.** In polyethylene kayaks view with distrust bulkheads that are held in place by any kind of adhesive. Welded bulkheads are watertight and help give rigidity to the hull.

8. **Rudders and skegs.** Rudders and skegs are fitted to kayaks to counteract the turning effects of wind and waves on the boat's hull and to keep the kayak running on a straight course. Rudders are operated by the paddler's feet and move from side to side. Skegs are hand-operated and move up and down. I prefer to use a skeg. If the skeg is controlled by a wire rather than a cord, set-

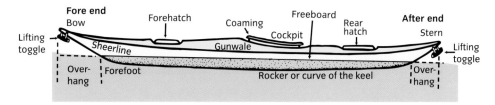

Fig. 1-1. Various parts of a kayak.

ting the skeg to the correct angle is very positive. Care has to be taken when launching off beaches that consist of small stones. Every now and then I get a stone stuck in the skeg box, and this is when the blunt edge of my kayak knife comes in handy.

Rudders, however, have many drawbacks. With a rudder it is difficult to get the firm platform for your feet that is vital to a good Forward Paddling Stroke. Rudders always break at a bad time or in the sideways position, and in following seas they tend to be out of the water when you need them most. Moreover, rudders are at their most dangerous during deepwater rescue practice.

CLOTHING

What to wear while paddling is a question to which everyone has his or her own answer. It usually takes only one capsize, however, to convince the beginner that it's a good idea to dress for immersion, no matter how hot the weather. Even if the water is warm, you will soon be chilled when paddling in wet clothing into a 3-knot wind (that's the speed you are moving through the air as you paddle along). For my own part, even when flat-water paddling off the coast of Florida, I always wear a pair of high-waisted, neoprene shorts under my T-shirt—the shorts come up under my chest. If it starts to rain, I can always add extra clothing to this combination while I am on the water.

What I have tried to do in the following sections is to give you, as a novice, some guidance as to the basic options of what to wear for your comfort and safety.

The best garments to put next to your skin are those that do not absorb moisture but instead allow your perspiration to evaporate away quickly. Impermeable, woven fabrics such as *polyester* or *polypropylene* are the best. These materials are usually referred to under the general heading of *"polypro."* Wool is also a good material, as the fibers trap heat even when they get wet. (Have you ever heard of a sheep suffering from hypothermia?) Cotton, unfortunately, is just the opposite: It absorbs moisture, is a poor insulator, and, when it gets wet, is slow to dry. For these reasons, therefore, cotton is suitable only for hot climates and warm water.

One of the wonderful discoveries you will make is that, apart from in the tropics, the air you paddle through is much warmer than the water you paddle over. The difference can often be as much as 30 degrees. Your clothing, therefore, should also give you insulation, in the event of a capsize, as well as protection from the wind and spray while you are on the move. Since most of us paddle in an environment where the water is cold and the air is warm, it is difficult to find a suitable mode of dress that will keep you from becoming hypothermic in the water but prevent you from overheating or getting chilled while you are paddling. As a novice, you will be experimenting with the various paddling techniques and rescues described in this book. So it is safe to assume that you will capsize at some time or another. If you wear the correct clothing, these capsizes should affect you no more than is the case when a skier who is learning to ski falls down in the snow. You merely get up, dust yourself off, and try again. In your case, you'll merely have to wring yourself out!

Immersion Clothing

Two types of garment—the wet suit and the dry suit—are specifically designed to keep paddlers and other water-sports practitioners warm during prolonged exposure to or immersion in cold water.

Wet Suit

The most popular piece of immersion clothing for kayakers is the *neoprene* long john. These are made from $\frac{1}{8}$ to $\frac{3}{16}$-inch-thick neoprene—that's the closed-cell rubber material that divers' wet suits are made from. Like all wet-suit garments, your long john should be snug fitting but not too tight. A properly fitting wet suit will protect your body from the dangers and discomfort of cold-water immersion. It does this by allowing a tiny amount of water to seep in next to your skin. This water does not circulate, so your body has time to heat it up. This gives you the sensation that you are swimming in a warm bath. Because your arms are free, you can paddle or swim without feeling that you are in some kind of straitjacket.

If your kayaking takes you to semitropical areas, you might consider a long john with short legs (is this a "short john"?). A T-shirt worn underneath either "john" should prevent any tendency to chafe under the armholes. In cold climates your undergarment should be made of polypro.

Dry Suit

A dry suit is an outer garment made of thin, completely watertight material with rubber seals at the wrist and ankles. Because the suit is watertight, any kind of clothing worn underneath will remain completely dry.

I own a two-piece dry suit. The top is joined to the high-waisted trousers by a watertight seal. This suit gives me a great deal of versatility. It gives me another dry top I can wear in conjunction with my wet-suit bottoms. Or I can wear the high-waisted dry-suit bottoms with an ordinary paddling jacket.

Warning: If you live in an area that makes the wearing of immersion clothing necessary, do not be fooled by the warmth of a sunny day. Put your wet suit, dry suit, or special combination on *before* you set off. *If you capsize, you will not be able to put these garments on in the water.*

Hats

Wear a hat. The hat should protect you from prevailing conditions and should not blow off in the wind. It is an added bonus if the hat floats.

Footwear

There are all kinds of footwear on the market for the water-sport enthusiast. There are beach sandals in abundance. Bootees made of wet-suit material come with thick soles, thin soles, or no soles at all (socks). At this stage of your career, you must always plan for the inevitable swim, so you want nothing on your feet that will fall off, drag you down, or hinder your swimming. You might be forced to wade through smelly mud or walk over sharp stones or mussel beds, so the soles should be thick enough to protect you.

If you decide to wear neoprene socks under your old sneakers, remember to remove the laces. The loops of the bow can get hooked around your footbrace during a bailout.

For my part, I am a great believer in dry feet. For this reason, I wear knee-high rubber Wellingtons that are a size bigger than normal. They are very comfortable, they keep my feet dry and snug, and I can wear a variety of socks. "Wellies" are not recommended for swimming, but with your Personal Flotation Device (PFD) in place, you shouldn't have to kick your feet about even if you are in the water. Wellies come off easily in the water, but the best kind have a draw cord that fastens around the top of your calf and prevents this from happening.

Assorted Clothing Used in Sea Kayaking

The illustrations of clothing (pp.12–15) will give you some idea as to what to wear in the various conditions you may encounter. Each of these items is discussed in the following pages.

A. Hat of woven cotton. Usually sold in white. Most are made to float.

B. The ubiquitous baseball cap. Keeps the sun off your eyes but not off your ears.

C. Winter's woolly hat. Some of those sold in mountain shops roll down and form a balaclava. A balaclava will totally cover your head and this will keep your ears, chin, and neck warm when it's really cold. Can protect hands while handling hot pans.

D. Rain hat made of Gore-Tex. Does not absorb water and will prevent the nasty stuff from dribbling down your neck and chilling you. Usually made in dark colors, so is hot to wear in the tropics. The traditional fisherman's sou'wester is good for heavy rain while on land, but the back gets in the way when the hat is worn with a PFD.

E. Neoprene helmet. Wear this for rolling practice in cold water. Can also be worn under a crash helmet.

F. Neoprene vest. Should be thin—say 1/8-inch—neoprene. Wear it under or over a T-shirt.

G. High-waisted neoprene shorts. Mine are long enough to reach up to my chest.

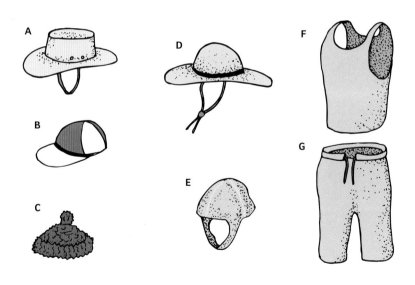

H. Neoprene long john. Make sure it does not restrict your arms. Some have reinforced knees for canoeing, but this is unnecessary for kayaking. Get a two-way zipper.

I. Dry-suit top. Secured at the neck and cuffs by watertight latex seals. Get one made of Gore-Tex. It's expensive, but you will not become soaked with perspiration. Gives watertight protection in the kayak when paddling or rolling. Remember, the waist seal is not watertight, so if you take a swim, some water will leak inside. The latex seals are expensive to renew and can be damaged by coming into contact with sunblock. Can be worn with neoprene shorts or long john.

J. Paddling jacket. Designed to keep out only light spray and light rain. Can be had with short or long sleeves. Neoprene collar can be fastened by Velcro. I prefer jackets with soft hoods and drawstring necks and lots of pockets.

K. High-waisted fisherman's trousers. These are loose fitting and come high up under your armpits. The front is fastened by a heavy-duty zipper and an overflap with snaps. Gives no protection in the water. Used by experienced paddlers in conjunction with a paddling jacket.

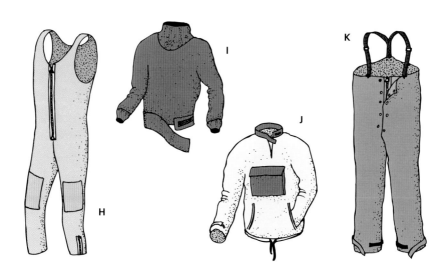

L. One-piece dry suit. Can be made of waterproof nylon or Gore-Tex. Latex seals at the neck, cuffs, and ankles mean that the garment is completely watertight. Any clothing underneath remains dry. Some have rubber bootees molded onto the legs. Entry is by means of a front or rear waterproof zipper. It is a good idea to have a convenience zipper fitted at the front. I have a two-piece dry suit. It has a multi- folded watertight seal at the waist, and the bootees are part of the legs.

M. Chota Boots. These modern mukluks are made with a soft neoprene body and thick, durable, rubber soles. They are the ultimate in comfort, either for pad-dling or wandering about on shore. An adjustable strap around the calf pre-vents the boots from falling off should you have to swim while wearing them. If you anticipate some water work and are not wearing socks, the lace-up system down the front of the boot allows you to tighten the neoprene around your ankles. To make drying easy, the boots have a removable inner sole.

N. Wellingtons/gum boots. These keep your feet warm and dry, and the thick soles allow you to walk over the roughest rocks and shells. Removable insoles are a good idea. The draw cord prevents the boots from falling off in the water.

O. Sandals with Velcro straps. These are worn alone or with neoprene socks. The Velcro can be rendered useless by fine sand, and the shoes can fall off in the water. I have known two cases where the straps caught on a footrest during an emergency exit.

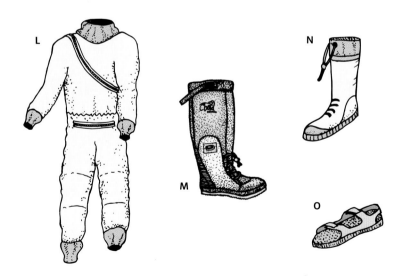

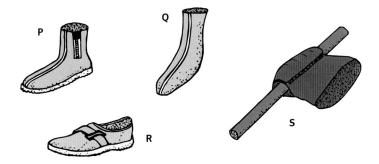

P. **Wet-suit bootees.** Made of neoprene, they keep your feet warm, and the thick soles allow you to walk over rough ground. Bootees are not meant to keep your feet dry, so in hot weather your feet will poach and the bootees will smell. (Bootees of this type placed outside a tent at night have been known to keep bears away!)

Q. **Neoprene socks.** These are similar to the above in that they keep your feet warm, but they have no sole, so it's like walking and paddling in bare feet.

R. **Beach runners.** Made of open mesh nylon, they sometimes have neoprene at the heels and toes. They are made to get wet, dry quickly, and are ideal for warm-water areas. They usually have strong soles, so they give your feet good support.

S. **Pogies.** Come in pairs. In cold weather your hands will need some kind of protection. Pogies fit round the paddle shaft and form a windproof pocket for you to slide your hands inside. You should be able to put on each pogie without using the other hand, so avoid tight elastic around the wrist. Do not wear gloves. You should always be able to feel the paddle shaft against the palm of your hand.

EQUIPMENT

Choosing the right gear is more than just a matter of comfort; it can save your life. Although equipment is widely available online, it is best to try out crucial gear, such as paddles and PFDs, in a paddling store, where you can try it on for size and get expert advice.

Your Paddle

Apart from the boat itself, the paddle will probably be the most important piece of equipment you will have to choose, and your choice is important. It is the paddle that will propel your kayak forward through the water and enable you to perform all the wonderful and diverse strokes and maneuvers that are part of kayaking on the sea.

The type of paddle blade I use is so important to me personally that on my frequent trips abroad, I always carry in my luggage two of my favorite paddles, specially made so that each breaks down into four pieces. When you are touring on the sea, you want a paddle that will allow you to paddle at a steady rhythm for hours on end. It must be mechanically efficient, and its design must minimize the paddle's tendency to flutter or slice. It should not be too light.

Your paddle should also be feathered—that is, the blades set at right angles to each other. I have always preferred to have my paddle blades set at 90 degrees, but once you become competent, you may wish to modify the setting to whatever best suits your own technique. However, I recommend that you begin with a paddle feathered at 90 degrees.

The advantages of feathering the paddle are:

- Feathered paddle blades are less likely to cause tendinitis (tenosynovitis or Repetitive Stress Syndrome). This is because your wrist movement is up and down and not from side to side, that is, forcing your wrist into its maximum (and unnatural) sideways extension of 20 degrees inward and 30 degrees outward.
- Feathered paddles result in less fatigue, because of lower wind resistance on the upper blade during the Forward Paddling Stroke.
- At the end of the stroke cycle, the correct exit angle of the feathered lower blade automatically places the upper blade in the mechanically correct position for a more efficient catch (see fig. 3-9, Forward Paddling Stroke, p. 49). It is the catch that marks the beginning of the next stroke cycle.

The Paddle Shaft

Your paddle shaft should be not completely round at the handgrip but slightly oval in shape. This will enable you to locate and maintain a positive grip for your controlling hand. Good-quality blades will usually have either plastic or polyethylene shrink-wrap at the hand location. This performs two functions: It gives you a more comfortable and secure handgrip, and it provides the paddle manufacturer with a means of securing the shaped former that converts your round shaft into an oval, 3 inches or so on either side of your controlling hand.

Buy two-piece, break-apart paddles. Doing so will allow you to fit a personalized handgrip if your paddle does not already have one. A two-piece will also enable you to replace the worn shrink-wrap covering when it gets scuffed. Paddles always seem to acquire sharp scuffs or nicks in the exact position where you place your hands.

Paddle Blade Shapes

As you can see in figure 1-2, kayak paddles come in a number of shapes and sizes. Asymmetric blades were designed in the late 1960s to give racing paddlers maximum power during the catch phase of the Forward Paddling Stroke.

Asymmetric blades are now used extensively by recreational paddlers and are sold in a variety of widths. I find that the easiest to control are those with a blade width of about 5½ inches. If you choose an asymmetric, you will find that some have a raised spine down the center of the driving face. This inhibits the flow of water across the surface of the blade, preventing flutter and increasing efficiency.

My own preference for many years was a Seamaster paddle made of wood. In the early 1980s I developed another design made of wood, based on the willow-leaf-shaped blade used by the Nootak and Nunivak Inuit paddlers. I called the design the Toksook Paddle (after an Inuit village of the same name).

In times past it was always accepted, and recommended, that the correct length for a paddle was arrived at by standing upright, fully extending one arm above the head and hooking one's fingers over an imaginary vertical paddle, and then measuring the height. Although this was fine for general-purpose or river paddling or for people of average height, it proved to be unsatisfactory in other cases. It was found that short people needed a paddle perhaps 3 or 4 inches above their maximum reach, while very tall people would paddle better with the top of the upright paddle level with their wrist. Because sea paddles are normally longer in any case than whitewater paddles, the variations become much greater. We now have a situation where a person, say, 5 feet tall would be quite happy with a paddle 230 to 240 centimeters, which would also suit someone, say, 5 feet 10

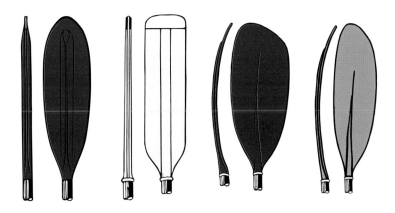

Fig. 1-2. Symmetric and asymmetric paddle blade shapes.

Paddle Size Table

HEIGHT	KAYAK BEAM	PADDLE LENGTH
Less than 5'4"	17"–22"	210cm–220cm
"	23"–26"	215cm–230cm
"	27"–34"	230cm–245cm
5'4" to 5'9"	17"–22"	215cm–230cm
"	23"–26"	215cm–240cm
"	27"–34"	225cm–250cm
5'9" and over	17"–22"	220cm–240cm
"	23"–26"	220cm–240cm
"	27"–34"	230cm–250cm

Fig. 1-3. Paddle size table. This table shows the range of proper paddle sizes for kayakers of various heights.

inches. I am 5 feet 7 inches tall, and I use a 240-centimeter graphite Toksook.

If you choose to use a paddle with a long blade—for example, a Seamaster or Toksook—do not be tempted to shorten your paddle shaft. If you do, you may find that you now clip the blade against the gunwale during the Forward Paddling Stroke.

Wing Paddles

As you wander around kayak stores, you may see what are called "wing" paddles (fig. 1-4), so named because in cross section they resemble an airplane wing. The blade has a broad, curled-over leading edge, while the bottom, trailing edge is extremely thin. Wing paddles are designed solely for racing, using what is known as the Olympic rotary paddle stroke. You may think to yourself, I want to go fast, so why can't I use a racing paddle for normal touring? The reason is that the touring stroke and the racing stroke are vastly different and require different training. One is designed to conserve energy, the other to make you go fast.

For the catch phase of the racing stroke, the wing blade is presented vertically to the water, a totally different presentation from the touring stroke. The blade is then moved outward, its dihedral angle causing the blade to fly forward with no slip toward the rear of the kayak and therefore no loss of power throughout the

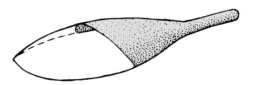

Fig. 1-4. Cross section of a right-hand wing paddle blade.

duration of the stroke. To maintain pressure on the face of the blade for as long as possible during this outward movement of the blade, the upper hand will be forced to pass well over the center line of the kayak and continue perhaps a foot out from the gunwale on the stroke side. This cross-over movement would be inefficient if performed using a normal touring blade. (During the touring stroke, the upper, forward-thrusting hand should never cross over the center line.)

Although the wing paddle is highly efficient for paddling forward, it can cause problems for the beginner trying to perform any of the basic strokes, including draws, sculls or braces. You will have only limited success, and you could well end up swimming. The problem is that in attempting some of these strokes, you will be forced to put the wing into a position where it could fly backward and very quickly pull you into a capsize.

Having said all this, if you want to go for a little extra speed in your touring kayak, by all means give the wing paddle a try. Keep in mind that because a high-speed cyclic motion has to be maintained throughout the racing stroke, racing paddles should weigh as little as possible.

Caution: If you finally buy a wing paddle, do not be tempted to immediately thrash off over the horizon at high speed. Athletes train for racing by building up their speeds and distances gradually. In this way, their heart beat and respiration keep pace with their performance. And as always, wear your PFD. (See "Warning" on p. 21.)

Pumps and Bailers

You are bound to get water inside your cockpit at some time, no matter how careful you are. I like a dry boat, so I carry a sponge to mop out the water from the inside. You'll find that you keep losing sponges, so tie on one of those brightly colored key-ring floats that marine stores use for advertising. If you feel you might have to remove large quantities of water, you can make a good bailer by cutting up an empty detergent bottle.

Of course, you could always use a portable hand pump. These come in various sizes and will remove about eight gallons of water per minute. One drawback is that you need two hands to work the pump, and, of course, you must also remove your spray skirt. Fit a flotation collar to your portable pump to prevent it from sinking.

Many boats now have pumps that are fitted at the time of manufacture. These are usually hand-operated and are fixed on the front or rear deck. Those on the rear deck have fixed handles, while those that are fitted to the foredeck have detachable handles. The mechanism used to work these hand pumps has also been adapted for the use of foot pumps.

The joy of pumps that come as part of the boat is that they can be operated with the spray deck in position.

Compass

Everyone who goes on open water should carry a compass. The best and calmest weather for kayaking often brings fog, and if you don't have a compass, you might have difficulty finding your way back to base again. As a novice, you need only a small compass. Position it somewhere underneath your deck elastics or on your spray skirt where you can see it and where it cannot move about. Fasten it to your PFD or to the boat.

Buoyancy Aid or Personal Flotation Device (PFD)

Your PFD (fig. 1-5) will be a vital part of your sea kayaking clothing. One of the most popular kinds has a zipper at the front and is put on like a vest or waistcoat. Your PFD should have a minimum of thirteen pounds of inherent buoyancy. Choose one that has a draw cord or belt fastening around the waist. *Avoid PFDs that are only supported at the waist by thin elastic.* A good PFD should have a waist belt that will tighten comfortably under your rib cage. This will prevent the PFD from riding up, when you are in the water, into a useless and dangerous position around your ears. Shortcomings like this are not obvious in the store, and the salesperson will probably not be aware of the dangers. Test the PFD in the store by putting it on and fastening it. It should not fit too tightly around your chest. Now get someone to pull upward violently on the shoulder straps. If the garment rides up over your chest and you can suddenly look under the armholes, it will be dangerous in the water. If you are in a store, ask to sit in a kayak wearing the PFD you have chosen. Put the spray skirt on and see if the PFD still rests on your shoulders.

Some PFDs have adjustable straps at the sides underneath the armpits. These are fitted so you can adjust the vest and allow for the various layers of clothing

  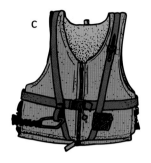

Fig. 1-5. Personal flotation devices: (A) A simple PFD with side zipper and waist belt; (B) A simple PFD with front zipper and waist belt, and a knife "frog" on the left chest; (C) An advanced whitewater PFD, which has a short tow line with a snap link on the right and a quick release at the front.

you wear underneath. Unfortunately, they are not usually successful in preventing PFDs from riding upward in the water.

My PFD has vertical foam panels. I find that these are much more comfortable and less rigid than those that have solid slabs. The vest fits snugly around my waist but is roomy enough to allow me to stuff my tow line and hat underneath if I need to put them out of the way quickly. I also have lots of pockets in which I carry all my indispensable items. In the United States, the Coast Guard has to approve all PFDs. Do not try to improve or stitch anything to your PFD, as this will effectively make null and void the Coast Guard approval.

Warning: *Wear your PFD at all times.* The water conditions and your swimming ability are *not* factors to consider. As a novice, you may wish to enjoy yourself with little bursts of joyful speed or perhaps by racing your friend—just for fun. You are untrained, so when you do this, you will be panting for breath. In other words, you will be hyperventilating. This means that you will be sucking into your lungs more oxygen than carbon dioxide. Unfortunately, it's the carbon dioxide that triggers your body's breathing mechanism, and hyperventilating can cause your brain to shut down and you to black out. So, you were a good swimmer. The water was calm and warm, and it was only 3 feet deep. And now you're dead.

If you think you'll carry your PFD on your rear deck, first try putting your PFD on in the deep end of a swimming pool—with a lifeguard or a friend looking on, of course! Then you'll see why it's simply better to wear it at all times.

Paddle Float

The paddle float is an inflatable bag that fits over one end of a paddle to help you reenter your kayak (see Paddle Float Rescue, p. 68). The float can also be home-made of rigid single-cell foam held together with tape. It can be stored on the rear deck. It does not have to be inflated and cannot puncture or rot with age.

Nose Clip

If you do not like water up your nose, a nose clip is indispensable. Carry it on a string around your neck. As time goes on, you will be able to dispense with this little item, but as a beginner practicing rolls and rescues, you will find the nose clip very comforting.

Paddle Leash

The purpose of the paddle leash is to prevent you and your paddle from parting company in windy weather or after a capsize. One end of your paddle leash attaches to your paddle and the other end to your wrist or your deck elastics, when the need arises.

Flashlight

If you get caught out and find yourself having to paddle during the hours of darkness, you are required to carry a light strong enough to warn other water users of your position and prevent a collision. Take care not to shine your light into the eyes of approaching boats. You will blind them and then run a real danger of being run down. Strobe lights are a bad choice because they are often used as distress signals and, therefore, can be confusing to other boaters. Instead, I use the type of headlight used by cavers.

PACKING YOUR BOAT

Warning: If your kayak is a new one and it is made of fiberglass, the first thing you must do is take the hatch covers off and leave your boat upside down overnight until all the nasty styrene gas has drained out of the watertight compartments. The gas generated while the fiberglass is curing is heavier than air and will linger in the enclosed space for many months. It will disperse naturally but not before it has stunk your clothes to high heaven, possibly impregnated your food supplies, and caused you to become quite ill.

Kayaks are designed to carry equipment, and you will find that one of the great delights of sea kayaking is the joy of becoming self sufficient and taking off into the wild blue yonder with your tent, sleeping bag, and all the rest of your camping paraphernalia. If you have ever done any backpacking and grumbled to yourself about the items you had to leave behind because of lack of room, you will find the huge space inside the hull of your new kayak to be extremely inviting. You can even succumb to the kitchen-sink syndrome and throw just about anything inside.

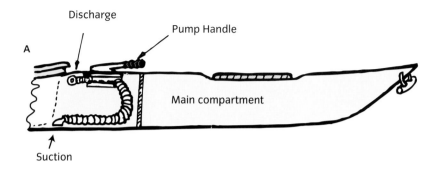

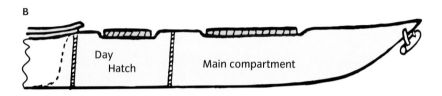

Fig. 1-6. Touring kayaks have different rear-compartment storage options. (A) The rear bulkhead is set back about 12 inches from the rear of the seat. This gives a large rear compartment and an unprotected storage space behind the seat. This space can be used for small day items, such as the first-aid and repair kits. There is also room for the workings of a deck-operated hand pump that would be used to drain the cockpit area. The discharge outlet of the pump should be on the side and not on the deck. The suction end should be placed behind and under the seat. (B) The rear part of the kayak has two bulkheads, creating two storage compartments. The smallest space or day hatch gives you the use of a sealed compartment within arm's reach and one that can be safely accessed while you are afloat. Because the space is relatively small, items can be packed tightly to prevent their moving about. If you capsize or for some other reason get water into the compartment, the space is too small to cause you any practical problems.

On several occasions I have lived comfortably for a month on the equipment I have been able to pack inside my kayak.

As a general rule, a kayak will carry as much as you can put into it except lead and gold bars. The heavier the weight, the lower the boat sits in the water and the more stable it becomes. You will be pleased to know that the loss in cruising speed caused by all this weight is negligible. Your acceleration will be affected, but for you as a touring paddler, this is not too important. How much you can carry will depend on the design of your boat and, of course, your own weight, but even for short trips it pays to work to some kind of plan. The following advice should help you get the best out of the space available and still maintain the inherent paddling characteristics and seaworthiness of your craft.

Day Trips

You may think that it doesn't matter how you throw your equipment into the boat for just a one-day outing—you have plenty of room, so why should you worry? Well, the first thing you do is to wrap your thermos flask or put it into some kind of bag. This goes for any bottles or round containers that will tend to roll about inside the hull as you paddle. If you don't take this simple precaution, the rattling, rolling, and banging noises will drive you slowly insane.

Try to keep all your gear together next to the bulkheads and then fill the rest of the wide-open spaces with the type of air bags that have long inflation hoses fitted. These will fill up any spaces and give you extra buoyancy and also prevent the stuff from moving about as you are carrying the boat or practicing rescues. Do not overinflate these bags on cold mornings. As the day heats up, the bags will expand and put undue pressure on the hull—perhaps even blow the deck off!

If you are fortunate enough to choose a kayak with a day compartment, you will find that all your bits and pieces can be packed and wedged in the space provided. Keep your first-aid and repair kit near the hatch opening so that you can get to them quickly in an emergency (fig. 1-6).

Multiday Trips: A Full Load

The heaviest items should be positioned close to the bulkheads and stored as low down and as near to the center of the boat as possible (fig. 1-7). This will minimize the "swing weight" effect and allow you to turn and control the boat easier than would be true if most of the weight was at the extremities at the bow and the stern.

Unless you are going to a place where water is scarce (e.g., Baja, the Everglades, or the Skeleton Coast), I suggest you take water purification tablets with you and treat natural water (rain or stream) as you go. Remember, a gallon of water weighs ten pounds. If you are forced to carry your own water, you'll find that small containers are easier to carry and disperse into odd corners among the rest of your kit. Large containers, because of their weight, should be carried near the central cockpit area. There is always a temptation to carry these containers between your legs. I have done this myself, but be warned: Doing this is dangerous. If you happen to capsize, the container will change position and it could prevent you from getting your legs out of the boat.

Large flexible or collapsible water containers are easier to stow than the rigid kind, because they can be positioned underneath other items.

After water, the next heaviest items are the stove, fuel, and the tightly packed articles such as the tent, tarp, canned or dehydrated food, and cooking utensils.

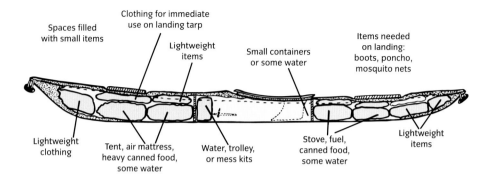

Fig. 1-7. Packing your kayak for an overnight trip.

I usually pack my tent poles separately, as it's easier to find a space for the tent's flexible canopy. Carry fuel separate from your foodstuffs.

It is important to prevent your gear from shifting about inside the hull, so wedge the heavier stuff down with lightweight clothing bags or any compressible items. It is not a good idea to store a large quantity of gear on your deck. It looks unsightly, will alter your center of gravity, and will become loose in surf, inhibit rolling, and fall off and float away during rescue practice.

Finally, pack your boat as near to your launching point as possible!

EMERGENCY EQUIPMENT

Sea kayaking is a potentially dangerous sport. Carrying emergency gear—to fix your boat, administer first aid, and signal for help—is not an option but a requirement.

Repair Kit

You should be able to maintain your boat and the equipment that you carry with you. The most basic item in your repair kit will be a roll of duct tape, and in the years ahead you will come to love the stuff. It will repair your kayak, spray skirt, paddling jacket, or hatch cover. If need be, it can even support a broken limb or make a stretcher. Carry some large safety pins. They will hold your PFD together if the zipper breaks. Wet-suit adhesive, needles and thread, and patches for your tent and sleeping mattress are also a good idea. You should be able to maintain your rudder and your footbraces. As your experience increases, so will the contents of your repair kit.

First-Aid Kit

Your basic kit should include scissors, tweezers, some small bandages, antiseptic dressings, some sticking plasters, and a good Swiss Army knife. How about a little book on first aid?

Emergency Signaling

When you need help, you'll need it quickly. Your biggest problem will be attracting attention and informing people that you are in trouble. There are certain options you can employ, depending on where you are and how many people are in the vicinity.

Whistle or Horn

The louder the noise, the more chances you have of being noticed. Ideally, you should carry a device capable of making a sound that is audible for a quarter of a nautical mile. You could carry a whistle fastened to your life jacket, although personally, I find that one of those trumpet-type copper foghorns has a far greater range and gives off a much more reassuring sound. Don't forget to keep it tied on.

Your Paddle

Extend your paddle above your head and wave it slowly, to and fro in a big arc. You can do this while you are in the water. It will be seen all the quicker if the paddle faces are painted a bright color. This is an international signal of distress and is ideal if there are other boats less than a mile away.

Flares

If you intend to carry flares, the minimum I recommend would be two parachute flares and two hand-held flares. The former will ascend to 1,000 feet and draw attention to your plight; the latter will pinpoint your position once help is on its way. A 12-gauge Very pistol with suitable cartridges is also recommended. Small hand-held miniflares, which perform a small arc through the air before hitting the water, are suitable only when assistance is close by. Smoke flares are useless in high winds.

VHF Radio

This is one of the best ways to summon help. (No operator's license is needed in the United States, but various rules and restrictions apply in other countries.) Emergency calls can be made on channel 16. You will say "Mayday" three times; give your position and the nature of your distress. VHF radios have a range of about 8 to 10 miles at sea level. The higher up you are, the farther the signal will reach. Pack your radio so that it remains watertight, and make sure the batteries are always in good condition. Buy a pretuned VHF weather radio. This is linked to the National Oceanic and Atmospheric Administration's (NOAA) national weather network and will give the weather forecast for the area in which you are paddling.

Cellular Phone
If you are in an area that has cellular coverage, why not dial for help? Pack your phone in a strong, clear, sealed plastic bag and dial through the bag.

EPIRB Type B
An Emergency Position Indicating Radio Beacon (EPIRB) will send out a signal on the aviation distress frequency. Your distress call is then picked up by a Search and Rescue (SAR) satellite and bounced back to a control center on earth. I consider the EPIRB mainly for wilderness paddling, and it is therefore beyond the scope of this book.

Make Yourself Visible
Choose your kayak and PFD in bright colors. Paint your paddle blades in a fluorescent color. Consider carrying a fluorescent hat in the pocket of your PFD. And buy a paddling jacket with a brightly colored hood.

CHAPTER TWO

Preparing for Takeoff

WHERE TO PRACTICE

You need to find a place where it is easy to launch and where you cannot come to any harm if you accidentally capsize.

Swimming Pools

Swimming pools are ideal places to make mistakes, because they are relatively safe and the water is warm. Pool sessions tend to flourish in wintertime. Sea kayaks take up too much space in a pool, so unless you are fortunate enough to have special short pool kayaks with rounded ends, you will have to use white-water boats. Most river kayaks tend to have pointed ends, so you'll need to make some buffers out of soft foam and fix them on the bow and stern of the offending boats with duct tape.

Apart from protecting bodies and boats, the rubber ends will also prevent you from demolishing the sides of the pool. Clean out any debris from inside the boats. Leaves and sand will clog the pool's filters, so if you want to use the pool more than once, make sure the boats are clean and the tiles undamaged.

Beaches

If the water is calm and the weather is kind, find a gently sloping, sheltered surf beach. Practice and experiment where the water is between 3 and 4 feet deep. If you capsize, you can merely wade ashore and empty out.

Swimming pools are a good place to learn the basics of paddling. Paul Hutchinson perfects his Draw Stroke, while the paddler in the background leans way over to practice the Sculling-for-Support Stroke.

Even the mildest breeze should be an *onshore wind* so that it will blow you back to shore.

Waterways and Marinas

If you launch from a dock, the water will be deep enough for large boats to come alongside. This means that if you capsize and have to swim back to the dock, you may not be able to stand to empty your boat. Before you launch, therefore, make sure you can get back out of the water again. Look for a concrete launching ramp or some shallow water with a trouble-free bottom. *When you are paddling, keep well clear of the main channel.*

Practicing Safely

Choosing where and when to practice and making sure you have company are crucial decisions in getting started safely at sea kayaking.

Beware of Offshore Winds

If the wind is against your back as you stand and gaze out across the water, it's an *offshore wind*. To test the wind speed, hold a handkerchief up in your out-stretched arm. If the material is lifted up and flutters out like a flag, then the

The coach stands at the center of the group during a dry land drill. Many mistakes can be corrected on land before the group gets into the water.

breeze is too strong. Do not risk going out if the opposite shore is any more than a few hundred yards away.

Paddle with Company

Kayaking is a social sport, so persuade your best friend to take up kayaking. You can help and encourage each other, but you can also keep an eye on each other. If you don't have a paddling partner, at least have someone watching your antics from the shore, and don't go out of their sight. *It is not a good idea to paddle alone.*

Furthermore, if you and your partner decide to go on a little trip, *always tell someone onshore where you are going and what time you expect to return.* This way, if you do not return, someone can call the Coast Guard to initiate a search and rescue.

If You Take a Swim

Don't worry if you capsize and have to come out of your boat (see fig. 3-1, p. 41). You know you can swim, and anyhow, your PFD will keep you afloat.

Leave your kayak upside down; that way, if you lose your grip, it won't blow away faster than you can swim. The air trapped inside the upturned boat will also give you support. If your kayak does not have watertight compartments or float bags, the act of turning it over onto its right side could swamp it and cause it to sink.

Next, grab hold of the nearest lifting toggle. If your kayak has a rudder, then you have no other safe choice but to hold the bow toggle. Fasten your paddle to the boat with the paddle leash or hold your paddle with the same hand as you grip the toggle. Now swim the boat to shore using a backstroke or sidestroke.

Emptying Out

Stand in about a foot of water and flip your kayak onto its right side. If you do this quickly you shouldn't scoop too much water into the boat. Now lift the *bow* upward and twist the boat *upside down*. Most of the water should drain out (fig. 2-1). Any water that is left can be removed by using your pump or sponge.

If you swamp your kayak but manage to swim it to shore, do not try to pull the boat onto land while it is full of water; the pressure will probably split the seams. To prevent this, when the boat is in about a foot of water, turn it onto its side. This should drain out most of the water. Now, with your friend supporting the other end, turn the boat completely upside down and seesaw it until it is empty.

Fig. 2-1. Emptying your kayak.

Your First Short Trip

So, you feel that you are now ready for your first big adventure. Let us say you are contemplating a journey of two hours to get to your destination and two hours to get back. At this stage you should assume your paddling speed to be 2.5 miles per hour.

First, you need to make sure that you have all the necessary equipment. Pack spare warm clothing, a first-aid kit (with your own medication, if any), an emergency repair kit (duct tape) for your kayak, and something to eat and drink—a hot drink in cold weather and cold liquid in hot weather. Take some group protection from the wind—an old tent fly or a tarp will do fine—and the rest of your safety equipment.

You will check the weather, the tides, and the capability of your companions and make it your business to find out if they know how to perform a basic deep-water rescue. Tell someone onshore where you are going and what time you will be back.

If you have chosen a nice warm day for your paddle, you might get some fog, so be prepared. As you leave your home base, check the direction in which your compass is pointing. Whichever way the needle is pointing as you leave, it will be pointing in the opposite direction on your return trip. In other words, if the needle is pointing out to your right as you paddle along the coast to your destination, it will be pointing to your left as you paddle back. Another precaution you can take as you leave the shore on your outward leg is to make a few stops and look around at the shore you have just left. Make a note of any hills, water towers, high buildings, or any other features or landmarks that will help you recognize the landing place. From out on the water, it is surprising how unfamiliar your home base can look when the afternoon sun is throwing shadows in a different direction.

Remember too that the tide has also been changing. Time your trip so that you arrive back to base at least two hours before darkness falls.

HANDLING AND LOADING

With practice, most people can learn to lift, carry, and load a kayak onto the roof of a vehicle single-handedly. Remember to keep your back straight when lifting.

Lifting and Carrying the Kayak

The easiest way to carry your kayak from one place to another is to persuade a friend to help you. One of you holds the rear toggle, one holds the front toggle, and off you go—but make sure you empty the boat first.

If your kayak is well balanced, you might find it less of a strain if you carry it by yourself. I know I certainly do.

For a right-hand lift, stand opposite the boat's point of balance. This should be an inch or so in front of the seat. With your legs slightly apart, your back straight, and the bow to your left, reach down and take hold of the coaming with your right-hand palm uppermost. Using your legs to help you lift, hoist the kayak up onto your knee and then onto your shoulder (fig. 2-2A). Because you lift the boat slightly in front of the center, the stern will remain supported on the ground (fig. 2-2B). Hitch the boat slightly forward until you find its point of balance and the

Fig. 2-2. Lifting and carrying your kayak step by step.

stern pivots up. Bring the paddle up to your hand with a deft movement of your left foot (fig. 2-2C). The kayak should rest comfortably on your shoulder and be easy to carry (fig. 2-2D).

Loading onto a Car

This is much easier than it first appears, because you are not going to try to lift the boat all in one go.

You will need a piece of old carpet to protect the back end of your car. The pile side faces down—this is important, as the burlap backing will damage your car! Lift or carry your kayak until you can rest the bow on the roofrack or the trunk of the car (fig. 2-3A). Walk to the stern and lift it high in the air. Now push the kayak forward into position on the roofrack (fig. 2-3B). Fasten the kayak to the roof rack with ropes or straps, then secure the bow and stern so that the boat cannot swing about. (Bungee elastics are not strong enough to hold a boat down on a moving car.) Do not forget your piece of carpet. You can stand on it while you get changed.

Note: If your kayak is made of polyethylene, the bars of your roofrack should be as wide apart as possible. This is especially important in hot climates because the heat can soften the plastic, causing the kayak to sag into the shape of a banana!

Fig. 2-3. How to load your kayak onto a car.

LAUNCHING

Perhaps more capsizes occur when launching than at any other time on a trip. The basic techniques shown below are not difficult, but attention to the moves may save you from a dunking.

Beach Launch

If you are launching from a flat, gently sloping beach, probably the best way to launch is by walking your boat to the water on your hands (fig. 2-4). It's very simple.

Place your boat as near to the water as possible without it floating away. Get in and put your spray skirt on with the release strap on the outside. With the paddle vertically in the sand on one side of the boat and your hand on the other, you can now walk the boat to the water by a hitching and shuffling movement.

Fig. 2-4. Launching from a flat beach.

Low Dock Support

This launch involves climbing into your boat from a low dock. Sit near the edge of the dock and facing the same direction as your boat. Place the paddle behind you and lay the shaft across the rear deck. Place your hands as shown in figure 2-5. Try not to put too much weight on the shaft. Most of your weight should be on your legs and on the hand resting on the dock. Place your legs into the cockpit one at a time, then slide down onto the seat.

I also recommend this method of entry if you launch from a sloping concrete ramp. Start by placing the boat completely in the water parallel to the ramp and then imagine the ramp is the dock.

Another way to launch from a shallow dock is to get in from a seated position. Merely sit on the dock. Put both feet in the center of the boat and lower yourself into the boat, keeping all of your weight on your arms (fig. 2-6).

Fig. 2-5. Launching from a low dock.

Fig. 2-6. Another way to launch from a low dock.

High Dock Support

This launch involves climbing into your boat from a high dock. The high dock support probably needs more care than any other method of entry. The boat is too low down for you to steady it with either your paddle or your hand. Personally, I always try to get someone to hold my boat when I do a high entry. First, make a little test. Sit on the edge of the deck with your legs dangling into the cockpit. If you can place the soles of your feet into the cockpit, then you should be all right—any higher and you might finish up in the water.

Sit on the edge of the dock facing the bow (fig. 2-7A). Prevent the kayak from drifting by placing your feet in the cockpit. Twist sideways toward the dock, keeping your weight on your hands. Roll over onto your stomach so that your behind

Fig. 2-7. Launching from a high dock takes the greatest care.

is suspended over your cockpit. Keeping your feet in the center of the boat, bend your knees and lower your self gingerly onto the seat. Your weight should be supported by your hands on the dock (fig. 2-7B). If your kayak has a small cockpit, you will have to sit on the rear deck before sliding into the boat.

Getting out next to a high dock can also be tricky. I usually position myself as close to the side of the dock as possible and keep my paddle fastened to the boat. With a deft piece of balancing, I put both hands behind my back, and totally unsupported, I slide out and sit on the rear deck. With the speed of light, I bring the nearest hand onto the dock for support. I then hoist my body upward onto my stomach, keeping one foot in the boat as an anchor.

CHAPTER THREE

On the Water: Basic Strokes and Maneuvers

CAPSIZE DRILL (OR THE WET EXIT)

I tell everyone that kayaking is a dry sport—and unless you are involved in surfing or some other such pursuit, it usually is. You should, however, resign yourself to a couple of capsizes during your learning period. You may feel a little nervous about the idea of turning upside down and coming out of the boat. Be easy in your mind—it's nothing to worry about. Imagine that you're out skiing and you fall down in the snow; all you do is get up, dust yourself off, and you are on your way again. I know that I was somewhat apprehensive before my first capsize. Like all novices, I felt sure I would get stuck in the cockpit. Happily, this turned out to be a groundless fear. The big problem is actually *staying in* the cockpit. Without thigh braces and some kind of padding, you will be pleased to know that you will fall out of the boat. Of course, it is difficult to convince novices of this.

Preparation

For your first attempt choose a piece of calm, sheltered water and enlist a friend for moral support. Unless you are lucky enough to practice this in a swimming pool, you should wear some kind of floatation device. Do not chew gum—it could choke you. To help build up your confidence, you might like to use a nose clip or a face mask for your first couple of tries. But don't worry—you'll soon discover that breathing out slowly through your nose will prevent the water from going in.

The Exit

Make sure that the spray-skirt release strap is on the outside.

- Take a breath and capsize. Don't lose contact with the paddle.
- Sit still until you are completely upside down.
- Locate the release strap on your spray skirt. It doesn't matter if you cannot open your eyes; most people find the strap by groping for it.
- Pull the strap forward toward the bow, then upward to clear the coaming (fig. 3-1A).
- *Lean forward.* Place both hands behind you on either side of the boat (fig. 3-1B).
- Straighten your legs, then push up and away in the direction of the small arrow (fig. 3-1C).

Once on the surface, grab the nearest of the boat's toggles. If you find you're not in contact with the paddle, then retrieve it. *Take the boat with you while you do this.* If your boat is caught by a wave, the toggles will, by design, allow your kayak to rotate in your hand. If, however, your boat is fitted with a rudder and you hold the stern toggle, the rotating boat will almost certainly give you severe head injuries.

Remember that if you let go of your boat for an instant, it may blow away faster than you can swim after it.

It is natural for you to feel a little frightened before your first Wet Exit. By all means, do the first one without the spray skirt in place. In this case, bang three times on the upturned hull with your hands before making the exit. Hanging upside down for these few added seconds will give you confidence so that you will not panic during the time it takes you to remove the spray skirt. It will also be a signal to your friendly onlooker that you have not expired and are in fact in full control of the situation.

Remember: The first movement of your exit is like taking off a pair of trousers—*you lean forward.* Nobody leans backward when they remove their pants! Turn figure 3–1 a quarter-turn to the right and you will see what I mean.

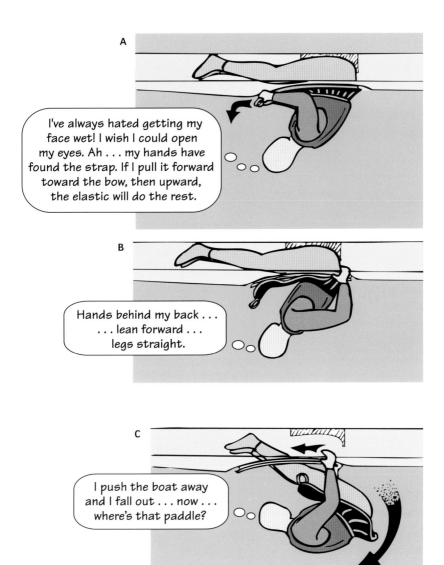

Fig. 3-1. Capsize Drill, also known as the Wet Exit or how to fall out.

PADDLES

Information on paddle types and materials is given in the Equipment section of Chapter 1. Below you will find additional instruction on paddle design and technique that will help you as you prepare to learn the basic strokes.

How Long Should My Paddle Be?

You will find a table of suitable paddle lengths for sea kayaking in the chapter dealing with equipment. See the Paddle Size Table (p. 18).

Left or Right-Hand Control?

To find the correct control position, stand with the driving face of the lower blade facing your feet (fig. 3-2). Now look at the upper blade. If the power face is on the right, then it is a *right-handed control* for *right-handed paddlers.* If the power face is looking the opposite way, then it is a *left-handed control* for *left-handed paddlers.*

Paddles are made with either right or left control to suit right-handed or left-handed paddlers.

How do you make sure that you have the correct control for your particular needs?

Fig. 3-2. Paddles are designed for either left- or right-hand control.

Holding the Paddle

No matter what strokes you intend to perform, the paddle is always held in what is known as the *basic paddling position.* (For the purposes of this book, I have assumed that the reader is right-handed and the paddles are set for what is known as right-handed control.)

- Hold the paddle with your hands slightly more than a shoulder width apart (fig. 3-3).
- Your palms should be on top of the shaft, with your thumbs underneath.
- Your hands should be equidistant from the center of the shaft. The knuckles of your right hand should be in line with the top edge of the right-hand blade.
- The power face should be looking backward.

- If your shaft is oval toward one end only, then that will be the grip for your right hand. Try this simple exercise (fig. 3-4). Hold your paddle at arm's length. Grasp it firmly in your right (controlling) hand, while leaving your left hand relaxed.

I am right-handed, so the knuckles of my right hand are in line with the top edge of my right-hand blade.

Fig. 3-3. The basic paddling position.

Drop your right wrist so that the knuckles are facing back over your shoulder. Do this several times, allowing your paddle to rotate through 90 degrees so that the left power face also faces the rear. It's rather like twisting the throttle on a motorcycle.

Remember that your right controlling hand moves the shaft by dropping the wrist, bending the elbow, or doing both at the same time. *You must never allow the shaft to move inside the fingers of the right hand.*

No matter what weird contortions you may get the paddle into, once you return your hands to the basic paddling position, the paddle should be ready for the next stroke.

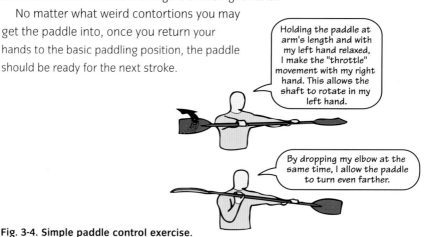

Holding the paddle at arm's length and with my left hand relaxed, I make the "throttle" movement with my right hand. This allows the shaft to rotate in my left hand.

By dropping my elbow at the same time, I allow the paddle to turn even farther.

Fig. 3-4. Simple paddle control exercise.

Paddle Blade

To make recognition easy, all the various parts of a paddle are distinguished by name. To help confuse the novice, some of the parts have more than one name. In figure 3-5 I have named those parts that are referred to in the text.

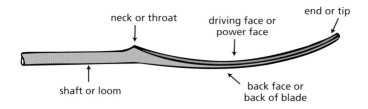

Fig. 3-5. The paddle blade and its many parts.

Leading Edge

In the following pages I make repeated reference to the fact that the leading edge of the paddle blade must be *high* for certain maneuvers. You will soon discover that if the paddle blade is moved through the water sideways, with its leading edge high, the blade will gain lift and act in a manner similar to that of a water ski. The blade will stay on the surface or at a chosen depth—but only for the duration of its forward movement.

You will see from figure 3-6 that once the leading edge is high, the blade becomes aerodynamic, and like an airplane's wing, it takes on a climbing angle and supplies lift and therefore support for the paddler's weight. As you perform some of the basic strokes, it will soon become apparent to you that a slight alteration in the angle of the paddle will give you support as well as propulsion. Eventually, all your paddle strokes will be *supportive as well as propulsive.*

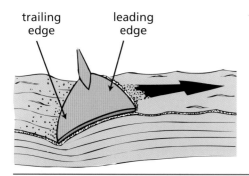

Fig. 3-6. How the paddle blade provides lift and support.

Extended Paddle Position

As a matter of course, it was quite natural for the Inuit hunter to slide his hands along to one edge of the paddle, thereby gaining extra length and leverage to help with the variety of strokes and braces he used as part of his daily work.

The modern paddler will often find an advantage in the added leverage gained by holding the paddle in what I call the *extended paddle position.* It will help to give you confidence when practicing any of the supporting or bracing strokes, and it is especially useful for such maneuvers as turning the kayak in high winds. There are also a number of Eskimo Rolls that require the paddle to be held in the extended position.

Figure 3-7 shows the extended paddle position on the left side. The cupped palm of the right hand is supporting the lower corner of the held blade. The left hand is a forearm's distance from the neck of the held blade. The knuckles on the left hand are facing *backward.* The outer blade has its *driving face* looking *down,* parallel to the surface of the water. You will notice that when this stroke is applied on the right side, the held blade will have its driving face toward you.

Fig. 3-7. The extended paddle position.

EDGING, LEANING, AND THE KNEE HANG

Kayaks built for use on open water do not turn easily. You will be relieved to know that this has little to do with your level of ability. The answer is really quite simple: Sea kayaks are designed to run straight. To make turning easier, you must lean the boat over onto its side so as to place the more maneuverable part of the hull (i.e., the gunwale) under the water. There are two ways of doing this: *edging* and *leaning.*

Edging

This is the most controlled method of getting the boat over onto its side, and therefore for you as a novice, this will be kinder on your nerves. For your first

Pushing Phase

Begin by moving your hip and the right side of your chest forward. At the same time, push your right hand forward at eye level, following the line of the gunwale. Avoid crossing your hand over toward the center line of the boat. During this forward push the paddle shaft is not gripped tightly but cradled in the curved hollow between the thumb and forefinger. The fingers are relaxed and curved slightly forward. With your wrist slightly dropped, push the shaft with the upper part of your palm (figs. 3-9A and 3-9B).

Pulling Phase

During the pulling phase the shaft is held firmly by the left hand. As this lower hand starts to travel backward, the grip changes to facilitate a pulling action with hooked rather than clenched fingers and a *relaxed thumb*. This grip change, combined with a hip rotation, ensures that the wrist remains in almost a straight line in relation to the arm (fig. 3-9C). Failure to relax the grip and swing the body will cause the wrist to bend to its limit. This is dangerous and could cause an inflammatory condition known as tenosynovitis (otherwise known as the "kiss of death" to paddling). The action of tightening and relaxing the hands "milks" fresh oxygenated blood to the muscles and helps prevent any tendency toward cramping.

Transition

Once the lower hand is pulled back to a position level with the hip, the upper arm is straight and the body is fully rotated forward from the waist. The upper, forward hand—with the paddle—is brought straight down to coincide with the rotation of the body and the lower blade being clipped from the water (fig. 3-9D).

In the instant before the right-hand blade touches the water, it is turned by a 90-degree flick of the left hand. In this manner the fully extended feathered blade will be presented almost vertically to the water. This part of the stroke is known as *the catch*. If the shaft is oval at the handgrip, this backward flick of the left hand will cause the paddle to fall into the correct position due to the cradling shape of the palm. This will not happen if the paddle is gripped too tightly.

The pulling phase is the most important in the whole stroke cycle. It is vital that the body and arm are fully rotated forward. The paddle must be dipped into the water cleanly, at boat speed and without a splash, in a position immediately outside the wave that runs from the bow.

The most productive part of the pulling phase is the time during which the immersed blade covers the first third of its backward movement. It is important, therefore, that the paddle blade is placed well forward. It is then propelled back-

Fig. 3-9. The Forward Paddling Stroke, showing all phases of the stroke cycle.

ward with a vigorous pulling movement involving the shoulder and hip muscles. As you pull backward with the paddle, *thrust your foot forward* onto the footrest on the same side. Pushing with your foot will give you the power to rotate your upper body backward and therefore place your upper arm in the correct position for the next catch. The pulling action ends when the lower hand is level with the hips. The speed with which this pulling blade is lifted from the water is also governed by the rotation of the body.

When worn by the paddler, the kayak is propelled not only by the movement of the trunk and arms but by the *whole body* right to the tips of the toes.

You must have a firm footrest to paddle your kayak forward efficiently. Without a firm platform for your feet, you will be forced to brace with your thighs. You will soon find that bracing with your thighs is both mechanically inefficient and painful, as it can cause poor circulation, sensations of pins and needles, and, eventually, severe cramping.

BRACING STROKES

The moment that you, as a beginner, realize a capsize is imminent, you will instinctively drop your paddle and clutch the side of your boat in nervous desperation. This is a natural movement. Unfortunately, it is not the correct one. You think, mistakenly, that your kayak is the only solid thing in a moving, watery, unstable world. It is in fact *the paddle* that would have been your means of support; and it is the area of the paddle blade, pressed onto the water, that would have prevented your capsize.

Stationary High Brace

The aim of this stroke is to recover the balance of the kayak from a potential capsize situation by using the driving face of the paddle.

In order for you to gain confidence, hold your paddle in the extended paddle position, *driving face down*. Lean over until you are off-balance (fig. 3-10). Yes, I know this is a little nerve-wracking. As you go over, the knee on your high side should be hooked against the underside of the cockpit coaming. Only when you are completely off-balance do you bring the paddle down smartly onto the surface of the water. As you feel the capsize halted by the downward pull of the paddle, push forward hard with your lower foot and flick your kayak back into the upright position using your hips and your upper knee. (This last maneuver is called the Hip Flick.) At the same time, with a motorcycle-throttle movement forward, turn the blade through 90 degrees and slice it upward out of the water.

Another method of bracing the kayak is merely to lay the extended paddle *on the surface of the water*. I tell my students to make a depth-charge noise by pulling the blade suddenly and violently downward. The blade hardly sinks at all,

Fig. 3-10. The Stationary High Brace in extended paddle position.

but the resulting "platoosh" sound and the sudden halt to the paddle's downward motion let them feel the pressure buildup under the blade so that they know they are getting the support they need from the paddle.

With a small amount of practice, you should be able to lean the hull over until about 2 inches of your spray skirt is underwater. Eventually you will be dipping your face in the water, but at this stage a wet spray skirt is enough to allow you to move on to the next stage.

The paddle is now held in the normal paddling position: *The driving face is still looking downward.* Your upper wrist should be tilted backward, with your palm facing upward. The best results are achieved by starting the downward stroke very slightly in front of you and then striking downward and backward (fig. 3-11).

Fig. 3-11. The Stationary High Brace in normal paddle position, another bracing option.

Stationary Low Brace

Slight corrections to balance—such as you might need if you are sitting in an unstable boat or are bracing into a small wave—can be achieved by presenting the *back of the blade* to the water. This is known as the Low Brace. During the downward push of this stroke, your knuckles should be facing the water. Once the boat has been steadied, the submerged paddle blade is taken from the water by rolling the knuckles backward in the "throttle" movement.

Sculling Brace

The aim of the Sculling Brace (also known as "sculling for support") is to steady or hold the kayak in a controlled lean at any angle. This means that no matter what the condition of the sea around you, your kayak can be held in a state of continued support. If the threat is prolonged—as for example in a tidal overfall or the sudden violent winds caused by a squall—the defensive angle can be maintained by sculling into the oncoming waves or wind. If you are knocked or blown over, you will find that this brace can bring you upright again. This stroke also forms the basis of many of the other kayak strokes.

You will see in figure 3-12 that it is the *power face* that is angled *downward*. It is the continual *climbing action,* rather like an airplane wing, that keeps the blade near the surface and thus provides the necessary support. All the supporting power is supplied by the hand and arm on the side of the bracing stroke.

To prove to yourself which is the controlling hand, try resting the paddle shaft in the crook of your elbow—I call this "elbow sculling" (fig. 3-13). You will discover now that during the stroke, your upper hand was merely supporting the shaft.

> This may look complicated, but the underwater shape ∞ is more compressed than it appears to be: Try to imagine that you are spreading the icing on a gigantic cake.

Fig. 3-12. The Sculling Brace, also known as sculling for support.

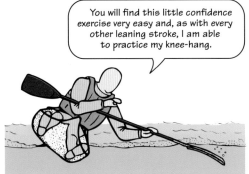

> You will find this little confidence exercise very easy and, as with every other leaning stroke, I am able to practice my knee-hang.

Fig. 3-13. The Elbow Scull.

For greater leverage and support, the paddle can be held in the *extended paddle position* (fig. 3-14). With a little practice you will be able to scull with your head lying on the surface of the water. In order to keep your center of gravity low during the stroke, you may find it helpful to lean back onto the rear deck.

Fig. 3-14. The Sculling Brace in extended paddle position, another sculling option.

Throughout the stroke you will be hanging on your upper knee and your lower foot will be thrust against the footbrace.

Paddle Brace—Waves

Probably the most important sea kayaking technique, with the exception of an extremely strong Forward Paddling Stroke, is the Paddle Brace. This gives you the ability to sit parallel to a breaking wave and stay upright. It is the key to sea kayaking. Once it has been mastered, your whole attitude toward bad weather and toward following and breaking sea out in deep water will become much more controlled and philosophical.

Low Paddle Brace

This stroke is of use when the waves are small and less violent. First, you need to find yourself a piece of safe sheltered beach and have a companion near at hand, even if your friend only sits on the shore and watches. Paddle out a few yards and sit sideways on a small breaking wave. Hold the paddle in the Low Brace position on the side of the approaching wave (fig. 3-15). As the wave strikes the side of your hull, the sudden jolt will try to knock you sideways in the direction of the shore. To prevent yourself from capsizing, *lean slightly seaward toward the wave.* Let your weight go over onto the *back* of the paddle blade and allow it to support you as the boat is pushed sideways.

wave direction

Fig. 3-15. The Low Paddle Brace is useful when the waves are small.

If you use the Low Brace to support yourself on a slightly larger wave, the boat may swing around, pointing its bow toward the beach. You will find that this change of direction has now put your paddle in the Low Brace Turn position. You can carry on shoreward, steering by this, or gently convert to a Stern Rudder Stroke (see fig. 3-24, p. 63) and then, by pushing outward, put the kayak back parallel to the wave and into the Low Brace position once again.

High Paddle Brace

To brace on a larger wave, and still within view of your companion, paddle out a little farther to where the waves are of medium height—say the height of your shoulder. Gather up your courage and position yourself sideways to an approaching breaker. Extend your paddle in the High Brace position and out toward the oncoming wave. The driving face should be *down*.

As the wave breaks against you (fig. 3-16), it will try to throw you over toward the shore. To prevent this, *lean toward and into the wave*. Place your paddle over the top of the breaker and lean on it. You will find that the paddle is supported on the upsurge of power inside the wave. Hang on, keep leaning seaward, and you will find yourself bouncing happily sideways to the shore, still in the upright position. *The larger the wave, the farther you must lean.* If you capsize, it will be because you leaned shoreward away from the wave or because you continued to lean into the wave after its power was spent.

Fig. 3-16. The High Paddle Brace is useful on medium waves.

REVERSE PADDLING

There will be many occasions on which the quickest way to position your kayak will be by moving backward. For instance, your partner may have capsized behind you and turning around takes time. Some vigorous reverse paddling will put you in a position to give immediate help.

For your first attempts place your paddle into the water as shown in figure 3-17. By pushing forward on alternate sides, you will move the boat backward. As an inexperienced paddler, you will find it easy to place the paddle into the water vertically—or in other words, in the slice position. Unfortunately, this is inefficient and paddling backward like this will give you no stability.

When you are paddling in anything but calm seas, the stroke should give you support as well as propulsion. For it to do this, the *back of the blade* should be presented to the water as *flat* as possible and at an angle of about 45 degrees to the side of the boat (fig. 3-18). With practice you should be able to swing your torso backward into a position to start the stroke, then lean over as you press downward onto the flat blade. Use this lean *and your body weight* to exert pressure *downward* and then *forward* during the stroke. As your body unwinds and you push your right arm forward, you must drive your right foot onto the footrest. Do this on alternate sides as you perform the stroke. It is only by using your legs and feet that you can obtain full power.

Warning: When paddling backward, *look behind you!*

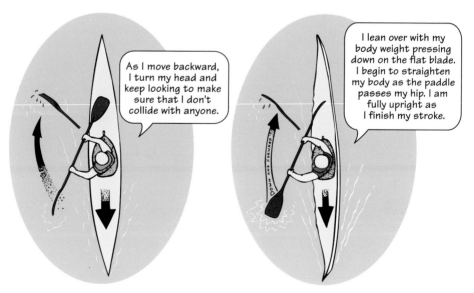

Fig. 3-17. Basic reverse paddling.   Fig. 3-18. Advanced reverse paddling.

EMERGENCY STOP

The stopping stroke is identical to the reverse paddle stroke. There are two stopping strokes (basic and advanced) or perhaps modifications of the same stroke. Your first try at stopping should be done with the boat upright, without leaning. Get some speed up by paddling forward. To stop, place the paddle blade vertically in the water behind you at an angle of about 45 degrees to the kayak's hull (fig. 3-19). As the blade submerges, push it forward against the pressure of the water, then quickly change your stroke over to the other side and do the same again.

The first two strokes should stop you moving forward. The second two should have you moving in the *opposite direction*. Do not worry if your first attempts send showers of water ahead of you as your paddle fails to bite the water. Keep practicing the basic stop until you can stop quickly without looking at the paddle blades and you are able to use your body weight to press downward on the flat paddle blade for a more advanced stop. Eventually, with practice, you will be able to present your paddle blade flat onto the water at the beginning of the stroke, in a manner similar to the more advanced emergency stop (fig. 3-20).

At full speed you will not be moving at much more than 5 miles per hour. However, the combined weight of you and your kayak gives the mass consider-

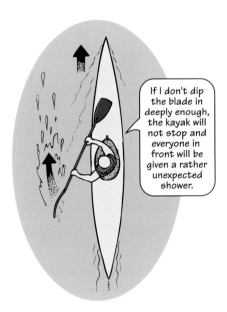

Fig. 3-19. Basic Emergency Stop.

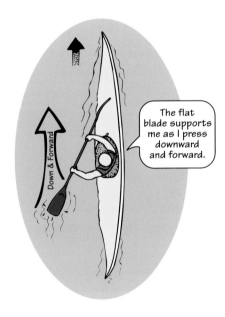

Fig. 3-20. Advanced Emergency Stop.

able momentum. To stop yourself moving forward, it will take four paddle strokes and a surprising amount of effort.

The secret to a good stop is in the legs. As your left arm starts to sweep the paddle forward at the start of the stroke, drive your left foot down onto the footrest. Continue to drive your foot forward on each movement of the stop sequence.

FORWARD SWEEP STROKE

The Forward Sweep Stroke can be used to turn either a stationary kayak or one that is moving forward. The stroke can be done either to avoid obstacles when you are on the move or to correct your course in windy weather.

The Forward Sweep is one of the easiest of all kayaking techniques and yet it is perhaps one of the most important. Because it appears to be so uncomplicated, many paddlers tend to perform it in a slipshod manner. If your technique is poor, you will be wasting energy simply because it will take more separate paddle movements for you to obtain the desired result. As a novice, you will prefer to sit upright during your first attempt at the Forward Sweep. In short boats normally used for river paddling, this is all that is necessary for a good turn. In a sea kayak, however, the stroke cannot be performed successfully unless you tilt the boat over onto its gunwale and thus cancel out the effects of your boat's straight or pronounced keel. To do this, your body must lean over as well.

Method

Lean forward. Place the paddle as near to the bow as possible (fig. 3-21A). The blade should be positioned so that the top edge is angled slightly outward. As you start to sweep out and back, angle the blade even more, *keeping its leading*

Fig. 3-21A. The Forward Sweep Stroke is used to turn the kayak.

edge high. At the same time tilt the kayak. Sweep the paddle out and around in a semicircle toward the stern. *Rotate your body* and pull the paddle around *with your arm straight.* As you pull with your arm, push forward hard with the foot on that side.

It is the angle of the blade that will provide lift and give you support. Your greatest angle of lean, therefore, will be during the first half of the stroke. Once your paddle passes the halfway mark, your body must start to come upright. Finish the stroke when your paddle is at an angle of 45 degrees to the stern.

Recovery

The method of returning the paddle to its starting position is almost as important as the main stroke. Your most vulnerable time is when your body is twisted around and the paddle is closest to the stern. To prevent any chance of a capsize, do not clear the water completely with the paddle when you remove it from the water. With a forward rotation of the knuckles, flip the paddle over onto its back face and return it to the bow by skimming it along the surface like a water ski. During the return the blade should hardly touch the water, but the paddle should be ready to apply a Low Brace Stroke for support at any time. If this return phase is done correctly, you will be able to maintain a considerable angle of tilt throughout the whole stroke cycle (fig. 3-21B).

Fig. 3-21B. During the recovery phase of this stroke, skim the back of the blade across the surface to return the paddle to its starting position.

Correcting Course

There may be times when you find it difficult to maintain a straight course due to a side wind causing you to weather-cock (i.e., swing your bows into the wind). To correct the tiresome problem, alternate your Forward Paddling Stroke with a Forward Sweep Stroke on the windward side. As you push your foot forward on the stroke side, remember to knee-hang on the other.

DRAW STROKES

Sea kayaking is not merely paddling forward and backward. There will be many instances when you will want to move sideways. Positioning the kayak for rescues must be done quickly, as time spent in cold water can be dangerous.

Basic Draw Stroke

In figures 3-22 (A-H) I talk you through the Draw Stroke as I would if I were demonstrating the movements to you on the water. Throughout the stroke the paddle is held in the *normal paddling position.* If you feel unsure and want to make things easy for your first couple of attempts, move your lower hand down the shaft and grip the paddle at the neck, where the shaft joins the lower blade. In this way you will get a feel for what the underwater blade is doing during the stroke.

Sculling Draw Stroke

Here is another way of moving the kayak sideways. Unlike the Draw Stroke, the Sculling Draw Stroke has no return or recovery phase. The kayak is pulled sideways by a *continuous,* vertical, underwater sculling action. Because of this, the paddle can be moved into position to begin a different stroke without being taken from the water, and the angle of the stroke can be altered to support the paddler in poor conditions.

Method

Turn the upper part of your body sideways in the direction in which you intend to travel. Hold your paddle as you would for stage C of the Draw Stroke (see fig. 3-22C). The Sculling Draw Stroke (fig. 3-23) combines the paddle position of the Draw Stroke with the sculling configuration of the Sculling Brace (Sculling for Support) Stroke (see fig. 3-14, p. 53).

You will knee-hang on the opposite side to the stroke, and your sideways movement can be maintained only by the continuous sculling action of your lower arm, wrist, and hand.

If at first you have difficulty getting the paddle to do what you want, move your lower hand farther down the shaft to the neck. Place the palm of your hand on the back of the blade under the water. This will help you direct the sculling action of the blade near the surface until you get the feel of the stroke.

Another approach is to start off by performing the Sculling for Support Stroke. Without discontinuing the stroke, gradually move the lower blade in toward the kayak. The supporting figure-eight configuration is now being performed by your *vertically held paddle,* and your kayak is moving sideways.

Fig. 3-22. The Draw Stroke is used to move sideways.

Try sitting on a stool or an armless chair. Place this book opened to the Sculling Draw Stroke (fig. 3-23) on the floor next to you. The figure-eight diagram applies equally to both right and left sides. Position yourself so that you are directly above the page, and then follow the movement with your paddle—either until you have mastered the movement or until your concerned friends have taken your struggling body to the hospital.

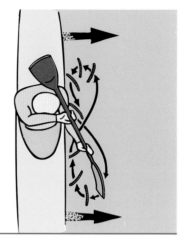

Fig. 3-23. The Sculling Draw Stroke is another way to move the kayak sideways.

STERN RUDDER STROKE

This stroke will give you a delicate control over the direction of the boat and allow you to steer the kayak while moving forward with a minimum loss of speed.

As you progress, you will discover that the Stern Rudder is one of the most important strokes in kayak surfing but it can be applied at any time when the kayak is moving forward (either when you are paddling forward or being carried on the face of a wave).

Method

The paddle is placed in the water vertically and trailed at the rear of the boat with the *back of the blade facing outward.* For the stroke to be efficient, the blade should be completely submerged (fig. 3-24).

- *To turn right:* Push the controlling blade *outward,* away from the hull.
- *To turn left:* Pull the blade in, toward the hull. The steering is limited on this side.
- *To go straight:* Allow the controlling blade to trail with no sideways movement.

When you are running with a following wind, you'll find that you have difficulty in keeping the boat straight. You can counteract the effect of small waves by incorporating a Stern Rudder into your Forward Paddling Stroke.

If the following waves are large and green, you may have to apply the correcting

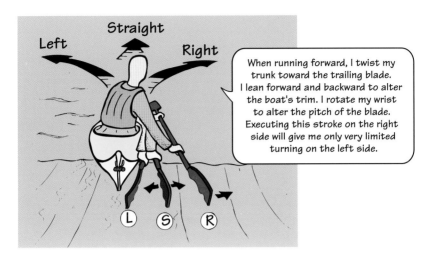

Fig. 3-24. The Stern Rudder Stroke enables you to steer the kayak while moving forward.

stroke more powerfully for a longer period. If the changes in direction are sudden, and the powerful "out-push" part of the stroke is the only way to correct, you may find yourself continually having to change sides. Depending on the hull shape, the turn may be easier if the kayak is made to *lean slightly on the opposite side* to the ruddering stroke. You will discover this as you practice in your own boat.

This stroke offers very little support, and the blade cannot be leaned upon unless the kayak is moving very fast.

LOW BRACE TURN (LOW TELEMARK TURN)

The Low Brace Turn supports the paddler and turns a forward-moving kayak.

Method

Paddle forward fast. Twist your body around to the right, and as you do this, allow your left knee to come up into the knee-hang position. Your right leg should be pushing down onto the footrest. As you do this, reach out with your right arm and present the back of the right blade to the water *with its leading edge high* (fig. 3-25). Your arm should be almost straight, with the knuckles turned downward. The angle of the blade is such that it planes on the surface of the water, enabling the paddler to lean right over on the blade, thus getting plenty of support. The left arm is passed in front of the body. The paddle is held at a *low angle to the water*. Throughout the stroke you will be knee-hanging with the upper knee.

Fig. 3-25. The Low Brace Turn allows you to turn while moving forward quickly. The greater the speed of the kayak, the farther the lean, the better the turn.

HIGH BRACE TURN (HIGH TELEMARK TURN)

The High Brace Turn is a turn performed in the High Brace support position while traveling forward. Once the turn is completed, the paddle can be drawn in toward the bow (fig. 3-26) and into a position from which it can be moved smoothly into the Forward Paddling Stroke. The High Brace Turn is both fast and powerful. Although the stroke's main application is in surf or broken water, the necessary movements can be practiced and perfected on still water. It is also an excellent technical challenge for the novice paddler.

Method

Paddle forward fast. Reach well out and place the paddle into the water with the leading edge high. Lean your body over and tilt the boat so that you are supported on the "lift" of the blade. As you lean over, knee-hang on the high side and exert pressure on the water by increasing the angle of the blade; at the same time push your lower hand forward and in toward the knee that is giving you the hanging support.

I'm told that my thumb is in the "nose-pick" position!

Fig. 3-26. The High Brace Turn is used to turn quickly in the surf.

Take note of the correct position of the upper arm in the illustration. The elbow is thrust forward, the wrist is thrown back, and the palm of the hand supporting the blade is facing upward. The lower hand is not gripping the shaft tightly. If you feel that your little finger is wrapped around the shaft, your handgrip will be hindering the correct paddle presentation. You will find it easier to place the paddle onto the water correctly if you allow your fingers to slope diagonally across the shaft.

The quality of your turn will depend on how fast the kayak is moving forward, on the angle of tilt of the boat's hull, and on the angle of the paddle blade to the water.

The coach watches his kayaking students as they practice their Sculling-for-Support Stroke.

CHAPTER FOUR

Rescues: Capsizes Away from Land

PADDLE FLOAT RESCUE

This solo rescue is directed to those people who find themselves in the unhappy position of swimming next to their upturned kayak, after having become separated from their friend or group.

Buoyancy can be supplied to the paddle blade by means of a float. This float can be either solid foam, with straps or loops to hold the float in place, or fashioned like an inflatable sleeve, with double walls. As the bag inflates, the walls fill with air and tighten their grip on the blade.

Keep your paddle float secured under the elastics on the rear deck of your kayak. Do not store the float inside any sealed compartment. Taking a hatch cover off during your recovery could cause the boat to swamp.

Method

1. After the capsize, position yourself on the downwind side of your upturned boat. This is in case the wind blows your kayak away faster than you can swim after it.
2. Right the kayak as quickly as possible. Try to lift upward as you flip the boat over; otherwise, you'll add to your problems by swamping the boat.
3. Slip the float over a paddle blade. Inflate the paddle float slowly (fig. 4-1A). Blowing quickly could cause you to hyperventilate and black out.

A

B

C

D

E

Fig. 4-1. The Paddle Float Rescue is a self-rescue.

4. If you have any prepositioned elastics or other fasteners, use them now and secure your paddle to act as an outrigger. If not, move on to step 5.

5. Position your body close to the side of the kayak, aft of the cockpit. Hold the rear of the coaming and the paddle together in the same hand. Hoist your body upward and hook your legs onto the paddle blade (fig. 4-1B). Bring one leg into the cockpit (fig. 4-1C), carefully followed by the other leg (fig. 4-1D). You will now be facing the rear deck. Keep your weight on the float side as you do this. Positioning your body like this is not as easy as it may sound.

6. This next stage of the maneuver is the most difficult. You must perform a one-handed rolling twist. Once you have rolled over onto your back, use both hands on the paddle to balance yourself. Throughout this contortion maintain a slight lean on the float side. You can now slide forward into the cockpit.

7. Use the paddle float to help you stabilize the kayak during the time you are bailing out.

It's a good idea to try all these movements in the correct sequence on dry land. Yes, I know you'll look silly—and feel even sillier—but believe me, it is time and effort well spent. Then, as with all other deepwater rescues, the Paddle Float Rescue should be practiced in controlled conditions on calm water, in the company of others.

Warning: I would like to offer a cautionary word here to the lone paddler, whose plans for any kind of future are based on the successful outcome of a

Pat leaves her kayak in a confidence-building exercise, while her husband holds tightly onto the boat. "I thought I'd never do this!"

Paddle Float Rescue. Although the rescue itself may work fine, it is merely putting you back into the conditions that capsized you in the first place. If you capsize when you are part of a group and you are rescued by your companions, there are several options open to them—even in the roughest conditions—for ensuring your safety. These options are not available if you are paddling alone.

Finally, *if you can't get back into your boat by any method, keep contact with the upturned boat at all costs; otherwise, your chances of being seen are very slim.*

"T" RESCUE

Let us suppose that you are paddling along in deep water with your friend. You are about 500 yards from shore when suddenly you hear a shout from behind. You turn and see that the other kayak is now upside down and your friend is in the water looking unhappy. Well, the good news is that with very little practice, you can empty the boat out in deep water and have your wet friend back in the cockpit in less than a minute.

The method I shall describe is for use with kayaks that have watertight hatches and bulkheads or have all the space inside filled by fully inflated air bags. Because of the position that boats take up on the water, this rescue is known as the "T" Rescue.

Method

1. Position yourself at the bow of the upturned boat. When boats are floating upside down, it can be difficult to distinguish the front from the back. Look for the two screws that hold the footrest—that's the front. The swimmer holds onto the stern and, with your help, lifts and twists the bow of the kayak so that it turns right side up (fig. 4-2A). Some water will be scooped into the cockpit, but that is to be expected.

2. Grasp the bow toggle and get your capsized friend to press gently down on the stern. Use the wedge-shaped angle of the bow to help you to lift and pull the front of the boat over onto your deck (fig. 4-2B). Your friend can help with a push. Pull the top of the bow over toward you so that the boat is now resting on the flat side of the bow, on its side (figs. 4-2C and 4-2D). The act of turning the boat over should drain the cockpit, and you'll be in a position to see this happen (fig. 4-2E, p. 72).

3. If you are fussy and you wish to remove that extra drop of water, haul the kayak farther over your deck and twist it completely upside down.

4. Now that the kayak is empty, turn it over onto its right side and slide it back into the water. It is now time to get your friend back into the boat.

Fig. 4-2. The "T" Rescue allows you to help a friend empty out his boat in deep water and assist him in getting back into the cockpit. (Continued on next page.)

E

Fig. 4-2. The "T" Rescue.

Reentry

1. The emptied kayak is now alongside (fig. 4-3).

2. Make sure it is facing in the opposite direction.

3. Lay the paddles across in front of you, and grasp the front of the coaming as shown.

4. When the swimmer is positioned between the boats and facing you, give that individual the following instructions:

> "Come well forward toward me. Put one hand in the center behind your cockpit. The other hand is pressing down on my deck.

> "Let your head go back to touch the water. Place one leg into the cockpit and, using your arms, lift your behind upward and get the other foot into the cockpit.

> "Now wriggle and pull yourself in and onto the seat by pressing downward with your hands."

Fig. 4-3. Reentry into the cockpit during the "T" Rescue.

5. As the swimmer tries to get back in, the boats will be pushed apart. The rescuer needs strength and determination to hold the boats together—the heavier the swimmer, the more determination and strength.

6. Once your partner is back in place, hold the boat firm while the spray skirt is put back in place. Reseated paddlers will always feel a little unstable, so give them plenty of support while they are putting their spray skirt back on.

Warning: Remember, this method of rescue is suitable only for boats that are fitted with watertight hatches and bulkheads or are filled completely with buoyancy. Turning a kayak over from the inverted position while in the water can cause it to swamp and sink. Instead, boats with inadequate buoyancy should not be righted but pulled across the rescue craft in the inverted position. The kayak is then pulled right over so that it forms an X with the rescue boat. The rescuer then drains out the water inside with a slow seesaw movement. The boat is then turned on its right side and slid back into the water. This rescue, known as the TX Rescue, can be fraught with difficulties and is beyond the scope of this book.

After a Capsize

Your friend may have capsized through carelessness, in which case there is little to worry about. If, however, the poor unfortunate capsized because of instability brought about by the sea condition, then you have a problem. Remember, you are only putting your friend back into the situation that caused a capsize in the first place. It is important that you get the person to shore or into calmer water as soon as possible without another capsize. Use the Two-Person Supported Tow.

Two-Person Supported Tow

In a Two-Person Supported Tow (fig. 4-4), you should fasten a line onto the bow of the boat being towed. Keep the tow line short so that you are able to paddle while the unsteady paddler holds onto your rear deck for support.

Of course, I presume you will carry your tow line at all times, but for short tows this can be troublesome and unwieldy. I would suggest that you carry a short piece of line in the pocket of your life jacket for just such an occasion. To make fastening onto the towboat quicker and less troublesome, you may decide to incorporate spring clips or shackles on the ends of your mini tow line. Leave a little extra line on this connection so that length can be altered to suit different kayaks.

When you tow, you will need enough space to get your paddle into the water and yet still allow your friend to hang onto your rear deck. Towing from your waist will probably put your companion too far back to reach your rear deck. You will

Fig. 4-4. The Two-Person Supported Tow allows you to tow a friend to shore.

find a good anchor point immediately in front of you, where your deck line fastens onto the deck fitting.

Using a Waist-belt Tow Line

Feed out enough line to reach forward, fasten to your deck line, and then reach back to the kayak.

Before you clip onto the kayak to be towed, release the waist belt on your tow line and tuck the whole lot under the deck elastics. If you accidentally capsize, you do not want the wet exit hampered by your own tow line.

Close-up towing on the side like this can be a slow and laborious business. You will find that it's almost impossible to get a full stroke on the towside, and you will probably bruise your arm and bang your elbow. The good news is that you should be moving toward calmer conditions, so forward progress should get easier as you become more tired.

ESKIMO RESCUE

One quick way to prevent having to swim in the event of a capsize is to take advantage of a friend's help. This kind of rescue is known as the Eskimo Rescue and is quite easy. To make sure your friend knows what to do, practice this in a swimming pool or very close to shore in calm water before you attempt to do it in a real situation.

When you capsize, the first thing you must do is attract attention to yourself. Lean forward, and bang hard, quickly, four times with both hands on your upturned hull. Your friend will now paddle in toward you and present the bow for you to grab hold of. Being upside down and completely disoriented, you will have no idea on which side the help will come. To solve that problem, continue to lean forward, reach up out of the water with your arms and move them in an arc, first towards the bow and then toward the stern (fig. 4-5A). If you have practiced this successfully, you will feel the bow of your friend's boat hit one of your hands (fig. 4-5B). Now reach across with the other hand and pull yourself up to the surface using either the lifting toggle or the bow of the boat. You might find it easier if you allow your head to leave the water last and bring the boat upright with a flick of your hips (fig. 4-5C).

Because you will tend to push the rescue kayak away from you as you pull yourself to the surface, instruct your friend to keep paddling gently forward while the rescue is in progress. You will find that you'll have to change your hand position halfway through your lift to the surface.

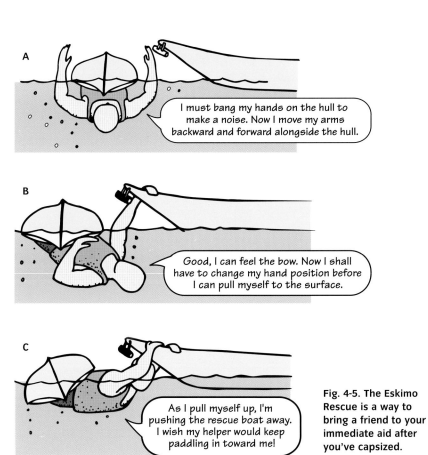

Fig. 4-5. The Eskimo Rescue is a way to bring a friend to your immediate aid after you've capsized.

While you are hanging upside down waiting, prevent the water from going up your nose by breathing out of your nose slowly. If there is no sign of your friend and you feel you have to exit, place your hands over your head as you break the surface. This will prevent you from being harpooned by the bow during a last-minute, demented rush.

ESKIMO ROLL

Some kayakers feel that the Eskimo Roll (fig. 4-6)—the technique of righting a kayak after it has capsized—is a basic maneuver. For that reason, I have included a teach-yourself-rolling diagram for the adventuresome novice. The roll is described for the right-handed paddler, which means that you will surface on the right side.

SUNK BOAT

I remember many years ago when I actually had one of the kayaks in my group sink. Now we all know this never happens, but on this particular occasion it did. This harrowing state of affairs has also happened to others. I have read of a number of incidents where, for one reason or another, kayaks have sunk beneath the waves. This has happened during rescues or when the boats have become swamped for other reasons. In a small number of documented incidents, the unfortunate individuals in the water had been abandoned. The excuse offered at the inquests by their "companions" is that they paddled off to get help.

Deserting a poorly dressed companion in anything other than calm, warm water will effectively sign the person's death warrant. So don't leave anyone— you can carry the individual to shore on your rear deck.

Rear-Deck Swimmer Rescue

Do not waste time trying to tow someone through the water by having the poor unfortunate hang onto your rear toggle. The drag is too great for you to make any real headway, and the person in the water will lose body heat.

Instead, instruct your friend to climb up carefully onto your rear deck (fig. 4-7). Tell your friend which side to use so that you can be prepared and stabilize yourself by *sculling for support* on that side.

You will immediately feel very unstable, so instruct your friend to lie down low on the deck and keep his *center of gravity as low as possible.* If the sea is rough, you will have to try to get some stability. To restore some kind of trim to your kayak, the passenger should be as far forward as possible, with his head touching your back. If the sea is rough, you will need some help with stability. Get your passenger to spread his arms out onto the surface of the water and let his legs hang

FISH-EYE VIEW

Open your eyes and breathe out slowly through your nose. Push your head and arms upward toward the light, in the direction of the small arrows. Swing out with the right-hand blade. The outer edge of the blade is tilted upward now as it planes along the surface. Keep the right arm almost straight. The left hand pushes up and out of the water and forward. As your head breaks the surface, your right bicep should have just brushed past your nose. Pull down hard with your right hand and flick your hips upward. Congratulations, you are now on the surface!

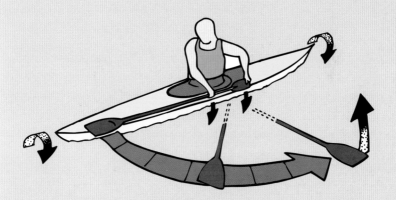

THE WIND-UP
(surface preparatory position)

Position the paddle on your left side. Hold the top corner of the nearest blade in your left palm, thumb downward, fingers inside. Your right hand holds the shaft a forearm's length down from the blade. The back of your hand is looking outward from the side; your knuckles are facing down toward the water. The outward edge of the forward paddle blade is tilted slightly down toward the water. Lean forward. Take a deep breath and capsize.

Turn the page upside down

Fig. 4-6. Practicing the Eskimo Roll.

Fig. 4-7. The Rear-Deck Swimmer Rescue enables you to tow a friend to shore after his boat has sunk.

down on both sides. You certainly will not be able to paddle very fast like this, but you should feel reasonably stable and you will make slow but steady progress.

As you struggle to paddle forward, you will soon get used to the dead weight on the rear deck and you may even feel confident enough to tell the passenger to raise his legs and use his arms as if he were paddling a surfboard. Your speed will increase now. However, you must warn your friend that if he gets the feeling that you are going to capsize, he must quickly spread his arms and legs out once again. If he feels that you are actually about to tip over, he must drop off to allow you to do a support stroke.

Warning: Carrying lightweight young people on the rear deck is child's play. However, if your kayak has low volume, the weight of a large paddler behind you will cause your bow to stick up and your rear deck to partially submerge. If you are unfortunate enough to have a faulty or badly designed rear hatch, the pressure could cause your rear compartment to take in water.

CHAPTER FIVE

Basic Seamanship

TIDES AND TIDAL STREAMS

You need to know something about tides and tidal streams, so what follows is some very basic information to help you understand what is going on in the sea as you paddle over it.

Let us suppose you have spent some time sitting on a beach enjoying the sunshine. You will notice that the water creeps up the sand until perhaps most of it is covered. Then, just as mysteriously, it all drains away again, leaving a large expanse of wet sand. What you are witnessing is the *vertical movement of the tide.*

Think of the moon as a big round magnet. As it circles the earth, it pulls a huge mass of water outward. This wave follows the path of the moon as it travels around the earth. Now imagine a jagged coastline such as that of Maine, with its hundreds of islands and inlets. As the tidal wave causes the water to rise, it pours in between all the separate pieces of land, filling all large bays. The sea forces its way through these narrow channels and up inlets and the river estuaries. It swills around headlands and gets rough and confused as it rushes over shallow underwater ridges as the water strives to equalize its own level. It takes just over six hours for all this water, known as the *flood tide,* to reach its highest point. For a short while the water stays at this height with very little movement; this is known as *slack water.*

As the huge tidal wave moves on, the water starts to subside. For the next six hours, all the water that flooded in now has to find its way out again. This means that the water flow is now in the opposite direction, draining out through the same narrow channels, around the same headlands, and over the same rocky promontories. This subsiding water is known as the *ebb tide*. The bigger the tidal wave—or *range of the tide,* as it is known—the faster will be these horizontal movements of water. This is because there is a larger volume of water to move, but there is still only six hours between high and low water. In just over six hours' time, it will be *low tide* again and there will be another short period of *slack water*, during which time there is no tidal movement. The whole cycle then starts again.

The times of the *high* and *low water* for all the coastal areas are to be found in books of *tide tables,* published every year. If you want some trouble-free paddling or perhaps even some tidal assistance paddling, buy a set of tide tables for the area in which you wish to paddle. Tide tables will also give you the range of the tide. If the range is only a few feet, you will probably not feel the influence of the water as you paddle. Some parts of the world, however, have tidal ranges of up to 40 feet. In any areas where the range is more than a few feet, you must take the tides into consideration when you plan even the shortest trip. Use them to your advantage; fighting them will merely be a waste of time. If the tide is running at, say, 4 miles per hour in the direction in which you are traveling, then you get a free ride. To attempt to paddle against such a tide would be futile.

Twice every lunar month, a little after the new moon and the full moon, the magnetic influence of the planet is at its greatest. The tides caused at these times are known as *spring tides*. At this time the horizontal movements of water will be at their fastest.

Changes caused by the vertical movement of the water can also be confusing. You may have launched from a beach over a few yards of sand. Five hours later when you return, you may find that you are separated from the narrow beach by a half-mile of weed-covered rocks or smelly mud. The good news is that this works both ways: Where you may have had a long carry to launch your kayak now becomes only a few yards at the end of the day when you are tired.

WEATHER

Knowing what the weather is going to do could mean the difference between just a bad day and a *very* bad day. Let us see what you as a beginner should be able to cope with. Personally, I don't mind rain, although paddling in prolonged heavy rain can be very chilling. It is the *wind* blowing across the sea that causes the real trouble. A gentle offshore breeze blowing from a flat, calm shore can create unmanageable waves a few hundred yards from land. The trouble is, these waves will not be evident from the shore. If a wind blows against the flow of a tidal stream, the sea will pile up on itself and create rough conditions. On the other hand, if the wind is blowing in the same direction as the tidal stream, the effect will be to flatten the sea down, but it might increase the speed of the tide.

It is also important for you to know what has the greatest influence on your kayak as you aim for a destination. For instance, if you intend to make a short crossing and you have a 20-knot wind blowing against your right side and a 3-knot tidal stream coming from your left side, you will move in the direction of the tide.

If the wind blows unhindered across a large expanse of water, this is known as the *fetch*. The bigger the fetch, the rougher will be the conditions. This is why beginners should stick to sheltered waters.

Of course, what you need is some kind of warning so that you know whether or not it is safe to venture out. You need to know when the wind is going to arrive, how strong it is going to be, and its direction. For this you need a *weather forecast*. Forecasts can be had from the Weather Channel on TV. The NOAA and the Coast Guard in Canada provide continuous radio weather forecasts. These can be picked up on some small AM/FM radios that include a weather band. There are other inexpensive radios that are tuned in solely to the weather station. Hand-held VHF distress radios are able to pick up all the weather frequencies.

If wind speeds of between 21 and 33 knots are expected, a *Small Craft Advisory* is issued. In these conditions paddle only on very sheltered waters. Gale Warnings are issued when winds of over 33 knots are expected, and winds over 47 knots merit a Storm Warning. Inexperienced paddlers should take this opportunity to go out on their bicycles.

It is a good idea to become acquainted with local weather patterns. For instance, every summer afternoon in the San Francisco Bay Area, 30 to 40 knot westerly winds blow toward the shore under the Golden Gate Bridge. In Baja everyone must be off the water by 10:00 A.M. because very strong onshore winds blow until late afternoon. Try to learn the weather pattern for your area.

ABOUT THE AUTHOR

Derek Hutchinson, an avid kayaker for almost half a century, is the leading international authority on sea kayaking. He is Coach Grade 5 in White Water, Sea and Open Canoe. In 1972 he was awarded the status of Senior Coach in the British Canoe Union and was for many years vice chairman of the National Coaching Committee and was its longest continuous serving member. He is a member of the Sea Touring Committee and the BCU's Expeditions Committee. Hutchinson  has also designed paddles and many of the world's leading sea kayaks, including the first fiberglass sea kayak to incorporate such safety items as watertight hatches, bulkheads, and fixed deck lines.

A man of many firsts, Hutchinson wrote the first book on sea kayaking in 1976 and is the author of several guides on the subject, including *The Complete Book of Sea Kayaking*, *Eskimo Rolling*, and *Expedition Kayaking*. Derek travels extensively in North America and Europe lecturing and teaching, and in 1998 he was featured in the PBS series, "Anyplace Wild," which aired nationally in the United States. His instructional video, "Beyond the Cockpit," is now sold worldwide (visit the University of Sea Kayaking at www.useakayak.org). He lives in South Shields on the northeast coast of England in a house overlooking the North Sea.

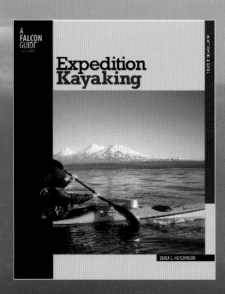